Contents

Preface

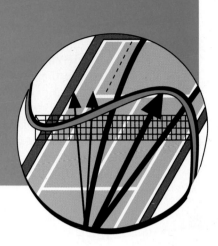

This is the third edition of *Game, Set, Match . . . A Beginning Tennis Guide* designed for the beginning tennis player. It is written for the student who is actively receiving tennis instruction, and who plans on continuing to play tennis as a lifelong physical activity.

There are several new features to this third edition that hopefully will enhance the learning experience of the beginning player. All chapters have been reviewed and adjusted where it seemed to make sense. The photographs and diagrams within each of these chapters have been updated, and they are now all in color, which provides a new perception and sense of the action and mechanics of tennis. All chapters have been revised and chapters on *Physical Aspects of Playing Tennis* (Chapter 6), *Mental Aspects of Tennis Competition* (Chapter 7), *Tennis Court and the Equipment Design* (Chapter 12), and *Tournament Competition and Resources in Tennis* (Chapter 13) have been revised extensively. In addition, the *USTA Tennis Rules* have been added in the appendix, a *Game, Set, Match Instructor's Guide* has been developed to assist the instructor in coordinating the use of the book with the practical experience of learning to play the game on the tennis court, and a new capsule learning aid, called *Cues*, has been added to the skill chapters. And finally, to add to the "new look" the material is presented in an 81/2 x 11 size to provide for easier reading and use of the book.

The chapters are developed in a logical sequence of learning experiences that include: basic tennis strokes; understanding of the behavior and rules that govern play; understanding of the game strategies; individual practice drills; coordination of mind and body into the mental aspects of play; and learning about court surfaces and equipment. Each chapter will assist the reader in understanding the game of tennis in a simplistic and clear manner. Photographs and diagrams provide visual samples of strokes, strategy, and basic concepts. Sections related to skill acquisition are reinforced with capsule learning experience suggestions, and with an "elimination of errors" review to facilitate an indepth understanding of those skills.

Tennis is a highly popular sport played at all levels of skill and by all ages. It requires a strong foundation of skill, and indepth comprehension of the intricacy of the flow of the game, and an insight into the rules of play. It is a game that is played at an intense level of competition by some and in a spirit of enjoyment by all who understand that tennis is a game. Tennis, as played today, is a never-ending learning experience for the player. It is a complex game that, when played and practiced over the years, becomes surprisingly simplistic and yet always remains challenging.

Game, Set, Match provides the beginning player with a visual and written analysis of tennis. Students will profit in their skill development by reading the descriptions of the skills and reviewing the photographs in order to gain a mental image of the execution of the skill. They also will gain from reading and understanding how physical fitness and mental preparation are critical to their improvement and development as a player. The two strategies chapters will provide a base for development of thinking on the court, and the etiquette and rules section will enable the student to make sense of the intangibles of tennis. There are also two informational chapters regarding the tennis court and equipment, and tournament play and resources that will aid the student in gaining a full understanding of the fringe parts of the game.

This material is truly a guide for the beginning tennis player who is taking instruction through courses or lessons and who will continue to grow with the game through the years.

James E. Bryant

ACKNOWLEDGMENTS

Since 1986 numerous individuals have contributed to the continual development of *Game, Set, Match* as reviewers, models, illustrator, and as sources to provide as accurate and complete of a book as possible. I want to extend a personal thank you to all of those who have in some way permitted me to gain from their knowledge and talents in order to write a book for the beginning tennis player that truly allows for skill development and growth. In particular, I want to convey a special thank you to my former students who have given feedback and served as a true test of the practicality and applicability for the book as designed for a beginning player.

Specifically, I want to thank those who have been instrumental in assisting in the development of this third edition. These people include photographer Eric Risberg who created the quality photographs that show tennis skill at its best, Richard Gonzales of the Cupertino Tennis Center, Cupertino, CA, who provided beautiful facilities for all of the photographs, Bob Schram who designed the great cover, and models Anh-Dao Ngyuen and John Hubbell, San Jose State University tennis coaches, who not only performed the proper skills to be photographed, but who also made appropriate suggestions that make the book that much better.

James E. Bryant

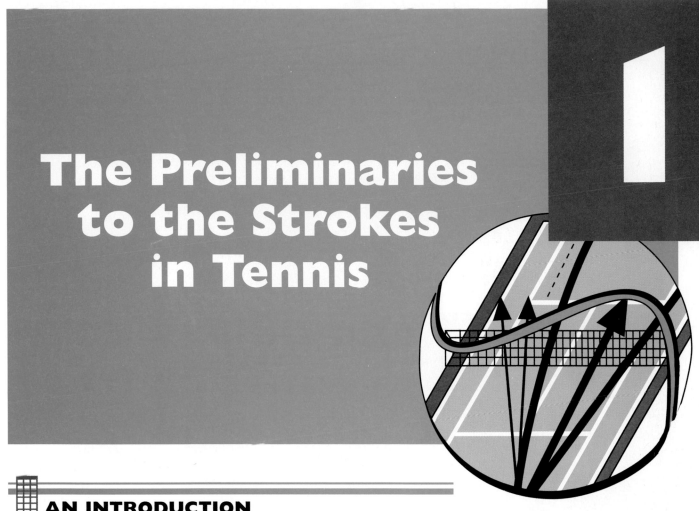

The Preliminaries to the Strokes in Tennis

AN INTRODUCTION

To play tennis, it is imperative to know how to hold a tennis racket for a particular stroke, and how to stand and move. Recognizing the spin of the ball, although not of immediate concern to the beginner, is extremely important as the player's skills develop. It is also wise to gain a comprehension of racket face control and have a feel for the ball as the racket impacts the ball. Learning how to grip and control a tennis racket, and how to get ready to hit the ball, arc skills that must be established early in the learning experience.

BASIC TENNIS GRIPS

The use of a tennis grip when hitting a particular stroke is directly related to the execution of that stroke. The selection of a tennis grip that fits the stroke is necessary to complete the stroke with acceptable form.

The *eastern forehand grip,* a universally used grip designed for executing the forehand groundstroke, is also called the "shake hands" grip (Figures 1.1–1.3). Place your racket hand on the strings of the racket, and bring your hands straight down to the grip. As your hand grasps the racket grip, your fingers will be spread along the length of the racket grip with the index finger spread the furthest in a "trigger finger" style, providing control.

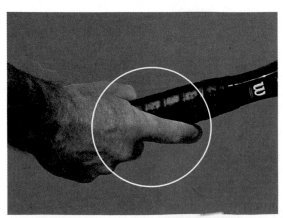

Figure 1.1 "Trigger-finger" position.

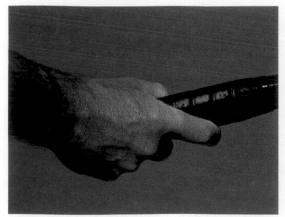

Figure 1.2 Eastern forehand grip (back view).

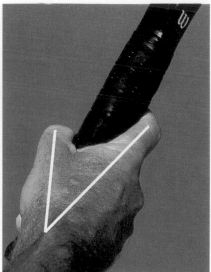

Figure 1.3 Eastern forehand grip (top view).

The thumb will be situated on the back side of the racket, and a "V" will be formed by the thumb and the four fingers on the racket grip. The "V" points to the racket shoulder when the racket is held in front of the player at a right angle to the body.

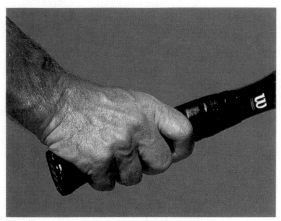

Figure 1.4 Eastern backhand grip (front view).

Figure 1.5 Eastern backhand grip (top view).

The *eastern backhand grip* is a conventional backhand grip used extensively in tennis (Figures 1.4–1.5). From the eastern forehand grip, roll your hand over the top of the racket grip and place your thumb diagonally across the rear plane of the racket grip. You should be able to see all four knuckles of the racket hand from this position when the racket is held perpendicular to the body. The "V" formed by the thumb and fingers will point to the non-racket shoulder when the racket is held in front of the body.

The *continental forehand grip* and *continental backhand grip* are essentially the same (Figures 1.6–1.7). They differ from the eastern forehand and backhand grips in that the hand is placed midway between the positioning of the two eastern grips. The "V" formed by the thumb and fingers points to the middle or center of the body halfway between the racket and non-racket sides of the body when the racket is held in front of the body. The subtle difference between the forehand

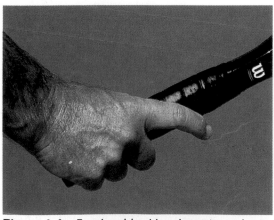

Figure 1.6 Forehand-backhand continental grip (back view).

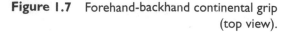

Figure 1.7 Forehand-backhand continental grip (top view).

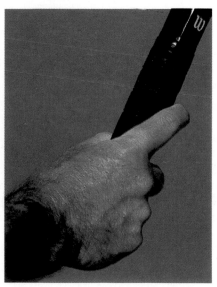

and backhand placement of the hands for the continental grip is that, in the forehand grip, the thumb grasps the racket grip, whereas in the backhand, the thumb is placed diagonally across the rear of the racket grip.

The *western forehand grip* (Figures 1.8–1.9) is often used by those who have received no instruction in tennis, or it is used for special strokes such as a topspin forehand ground-stroke. The grip is best achieved by laying the racket on the court and picking it up naturally. The palm of the hand faces flat against and under the back side of the racket grip. The "V" formed by the thumb and fingers, when the racket is held in front of the body, points beyond the racket shoulder.

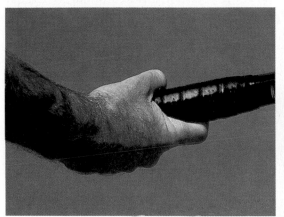

Figure 1.8   Western forehand grip (back view).

Figure 1.9   Western forehand grip (top view).

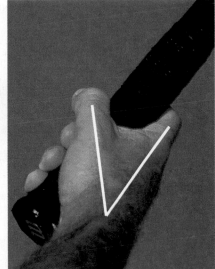

The use of the two-hand grips in tennis have become popular in recent years. The *two-hand back-hand grip* (Figures 1.10–1.11) is achieved when the hand on the racket side grasps the racket grip in either a continental or eastern backhand grip, with the non-racket-side hand butted above that grasp in an eastern forehand grip. The two-hand backhand grip must be a snug fit of two hands working together to execute the stroke. There is also a two-hand forehand grip that is used by a few players, but the grip is not widely used at this time.

Figure 1.10   Two-hand backhand grip (front view).

Figure 1.11   Two-hand backhand grip (top view).

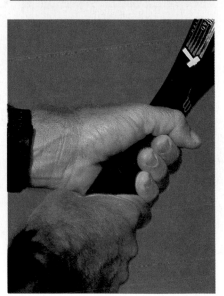

The selection of the grip is based on a particular purpose. Eastern forehand grips are used for the forehand groundstroke, while the eastern backhand grip is used for the backhand groundstroke and for special serves. The continental grips are used for groundstrokes, net play, and for serving. The continental grip has the added advantage of requiring little in the way of grip adjustment for different strokes; consequently, strokes are disguised when this grip is used. The western forehand is used with success when hitting top-spin forehand groundstrokes. The two-hand backhand is a useful grip, particularly with individuals who lack the strength to hit with more conventional grips or who are seeking more power and control for their groundstrokes. The disadvantage to the grip is that the player lacks reach for wide shots. The two-hand stroke is excellent for players who are willing to move and react to every ball hit to them.

From the perspective of *what grip to use for what stroke situation,* it is suggested that the eastern grips be used by a player who intends to stay at the

Remember: All grips require that the index finger serve as a trigger finger to provide control of the racket along with a relaxed and flexible grip.

baseline and hit groundstrokes. When serving, use the continental grip — it will provide control, accuracy, and power for an effective service. As a beginner, you may want to start by using the eastern forehand grip for the serve; however, you should switch to the continental as soon as possible. Going to the net to play a volley shot requires reaction and timing, which means that the grip should not be changed much for a forehand or backhand volley. It is recommended that the player maintain a continental grip for play at the net to avoid miss-hitting the ball and being confused at the net.

LEARNING EXPERIENCE SUGGESTIONS
Grip

1. Keep the fingers spread down the racket grip with the index finger serving as a "trigger finger."

2. Be aware of the location of the "V" in relation to the racket and non-racket shoulders.

3. Grasp the racket firmly when assuming a grip.

4. Understand the subtle differences with each grip and the purpose for each grip.

ELIMINATION OF ERRORS (Grip)

The Error	What Causes the Error	Correction of the Error
Lack of control of the racket.	Grasping the racket in a vise-like position.	Make sure that the fingers are spread along the racket grip with a trigger finger.
Miss-hitting a ball or poor execution.	The grip is too tight.	Relax the grip. Grasp the racket firmly, not tightly.
	The grip is too loose.	Tighten the grip. Grasp the racket firmly, not tightly. Check grip size. The racket will turn in the hand when a return shot has high velocity if the grip is too small.
	Wrong grip for the stroke.	Check purpose for each grip.

CONTROLLING THE RACKET AND GETTING READY TO HIT

Racket control is essential to good strokes and thus to successful play. Three basic actions are taken when swinging a racket that will provide racket head control and that will consequently accomplish a stroke. The basic *swing action* is reflected in the forehand and backhand groundstrokes and the various lobs. The serve and overhead smashes are described through the *action of throwing*, while the *punch action* is used with forehand and backhand volleys. By executing each of these actions or patterns, you will eliminate all extraneous motion, which will help you to simplify the action of each stroke.

There are also three basic *racket face* positions that affect the control and flight pattern of the ball, followed by the bounce of the ball on the surface of the court. The effect of these three racket face positions on the resultant action of the ball is dependent on the speed of the racket head hitting through the ball and on the angle of the racket face when it contacts the ball. If contact is made with the *racket face flat* to the ball (Figure 1.12), the flight of the ball will be straight, with the ball falling to the court surface due to gravity. An *open racket face* (Figure 1.13) will cause the ball to have a floating action in its flight, spinning in a backward motion. A *closed racket face* (Figure 1.14) will force the flight pattern of the ball downward due to the ball having a forward spin. Each racket face position is important to all skill levels of players, and understanding what causes the drop or rise of the ball gives the beginning player a greater insight into the total concept of hitting the ball and reacting to the bounce.

Figure 1.12 Flat racket face.

Figure 1.13 Open racket face.

Figure 1.14 Closed racket face.

Comprehending spins is a direct carryover from understanding racket head and racket face control. A tennis shot that is hit without spin is affected by three aspects of the overall stroke. First, as the ball strikes the racket face, a direct force is applied to the ball that provides velocity and determines the flight pattern of the ball. Secondly, that velocity is countered by air resistance and gravity, with the former impeding the velocity of the tennis ball and the latter pulling the ball down toward the court. Finally, the ball will strike the tennis court surface at an angle equal to the rebound of the ball off the court surface.

When a ball spins in its flight pattern, the tennis player must also cope with the behavior of the ball as it strikes the court surface. There are three *basic actions for balls in flight* (see Figure 1.15). First, *topspin* is caused by the action of the top surface of the ball rotating against air resistance. This creates friction on the top part of the ball, forcing the ball in a downward path. A second spinning rotation, *underspin,* is caused by the bottom of the ball meeting air resistance and forcing the ball to stay up longer than is normally found with a non-spinning ball. The final spin action of a ball — *sidespin* — is created when the side of the ball meets air resistance and pressure. This causes the ball to veer to the opposite side.

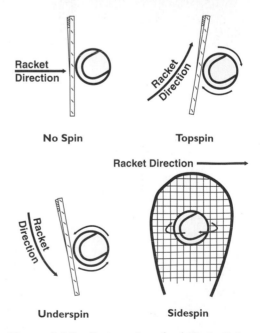

Figure 1.15 Basic actions for balls in flight.

The *action of the ball striking the court surface* is the end result of racket control action on the ball and the spin of the flight of the ball (Figure 1.16). As the tennis ball makes contact with the tennis court, the ball will behave in a highly predictable manner. A *topspin action* will hit the court surface with a high, deep bounce due to the forward rotation of the ball. A ball hit with *underspin* is usually hit with power and at a low angle, thus creating a skidding action as ball meets surface. The *sidespin* strikes the court with the same action and direction as the sidespin on the ball.

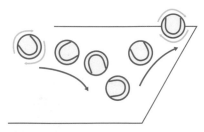

Action of ball striking court — topspin

Action of ball striking court — underspin

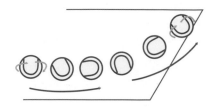

Action of ball striking court — sidespin

Figure 1.16   Basic actions for ball striking the court.

In summary, there is a cause-effect relationship to racket control and spin of the ball. A flat racket face at contact will cause a flat flight pattern and flat equal angle bounce off the court. An open racket face will result in underspin during the flight of the ball and a skidding action upon contact with the court surface. A closed racket face will provide a topspin ball action with a resulting high and deep bounce off the court surface. The player should understand that there is only a subtle change in these two racket positions for the slice and topspin groundstrokes at contact.

A closed racket face striking the ball on the side will create a sidespin action followed by a sideward bounce when the ball strikes the court. The beginning player needs to understand the various spins applied to a ball in order to cope with balls hit with spin, and to learn how to supply spin to various strokes.

Figure 1.17
Forehand groundstroke.

Figure 1.18
Backhand groundstroke.

TYPES OF STROKES

As an introduction to the preliminaries of the strokes in tennis, a definition of the *various strokes* should aid in a more complete understanding of the basic skills of the game.

The basic *forehand groundstroke* (Figure 1.17) is a stroke hit from the baseline following the bounce of the ball. The stroke is executed with a swinging action that produces a flat, no-spin (actually, a small amount of topspin is found in most flat shots) movement to the ball. The *backhand groundstroke* (Figure 1.18) is played under the same conditions as the forehand groundstroke with the same ball action. Both are swinging action strokes with the forehand hit on the racket side of the body and the backhand hit on the non-racket side of the body. Both strokes are foundations for more advanced strokes, including *topspin* and *slice (underspin) groundstrokes*. *Approach shots,* which are an extension of groundstrokes, are characterized by a player advancing to the middle of the court to hit a ball. All *lobs* (Figure 1.19) are also an extension of groundstrokes in terms of the swinging action except there is a lifting action designed to hit the ball deep to the baseline and with a loft.

The *volley* (Figure 1.20) is a punching action characterized by playing the ball prior to contact with the court surface. Both forehand and backhand volleys are usually played at the net, with *half-volleys* being an extension of a volley shot.

The fourth type of stroke is the basic *flat serve* (Figure 1.21), and it is described as a throwing action. Strokes that develop from the flat service are the slice service (sidespin), the topspin service, and an advanced stroke known as the American twist (another sidespin rotation). The *overhead smash* (Figure 1.22) is a continuation of the basic flat service, with the key parts of the serve reflected in the smash. It differs from the serve in that the ball is hit either on the fly or after a bounce on the court surface when the offensive player is positioned near the net.

Figure 1.19   Lob.

Figure 1.20   Volley.

Figure 1.21   Flat Serve.

Figure 1.22   Overhead Smash.

FEEL AND TIMING OF THE TENNIS BALL

The development of a *timing and feel for the tennis ball* is a prerequisite for successful tennis play. Regardless of the racket control, the spin of the ball, and various stroke fundamentals, the execution of each stroke is dependent on feeling and timing of the ball through *eye-hand coordination, timing,* and *focus.* Eye-hand coordination is based on past experiences of throwing and catching an object similar to a tennis ball in size. The swinging, throwing, and punching actions associated with tennis are fundamental to the ball games of batting, throwing, and catching that most American children play during their childhood. If you have played softball or racquetball, or have engaged in activities like playing catch, the game of tennis will

Figure 1.23 Position of ball and feet away and behind the ball.

be easy for you compared to individuals who have not had those experiences.

Timing is also related to where the ball will eventually be positioned to be hit rather than where it bounced originally. You must comprehend where the ball will go after it bounces, and set up behind and away from the ball so that you can step into the ball to hit it (Figure 1.23). Players tend to get too close to the ball or too far away, which causes them to lurch to hit the ball rather than smoothly stepping into the ball. If the ball is too far away, the player can adjust (and not lose timing), by stepping toward the ball with a weight transfer (Figure 1.24). If the ball is too close, the player should step away, yet forward, to hit the ball (Figure 1.25). The key factor in stepping away is the opening of the upper body as the racket is brought through the ball at contact.

Part of timing involves controlling the racket head speed. Players under pressure tend to swing too hard or fast, particularly with the return of service. You must remember to play from a relaxed position and control the racket head speed. The same experience occurs with hitting overhead smashes and groundstrokes when the opposing player is at the net. The added pressure tends to break down timing, forcing the player to rush through the stroke. The focal points have to be relaxation, confidence in hitting the ball, and concentration on the ball. Timing is improved immeasurably by watching the ball as long as possible. This is the part of focus that is most often ignored.

Figure 1.24
Stepping into the ball.

Figure 1.25
Stepping away from the ball.

The ability to *focus* is extremely important in tennis. The ability to "see" the ball and perceive the racket striking the ball will help the developing player improve rapidly. Being able to focus on the ball is based on the same past experiences as with eye-hand coordination. The recognition of the bounce of the ball in terms of height, the distance the ball is in relation to the player, and the relationship of the ball to the body are part of the focus concept. Additional focus points include moving to the ball, transferring weight into the ball at contact, and being in the correct position at the correct time. A final consideration is the ability to block all outside distractions and focus on the tennis ball as the only target.

The foundation for timing and feel of the ball rests with establishing a *ready position* from which to hit groundstrokes and volleys (Figure 1.26). The ready position is the first actual skill presented for the developing player, and it is the foundation for all strokes.

The feet should be spaced slightly wider than shoulder width and should be parallel to each other. The knees are slightly bent, and the weight of the body is centered over the balls of the feet. The buttocks should be "down," with the upper body leaning slightly forward in a straight alignment. The head should be "up," looking toward the ball on the opposite side of the net. The racket is held "up" with a forehand grip on the handle, with the non-racket hand lightly touching the throat of the racket. The racket head is above the hands, and the elbows are clear of the body.

The ready position gives the player the opportunity to move equally to the right or left, as well as advance forward or retreat backward. The first response from a player in the ready position is to immediately rotate the shoulders when the direction of the ball from across the net is recognized (Figures 1.27–1.28). A player with good mobility will be able to move the feet quickly from the ready position. If a player can be relaxed in a ready position, keep the weight on the balls of the feet, and then react to the approaching ball with an early turn of the shoulders and quick foot movement, the stroke has been initiated positively.

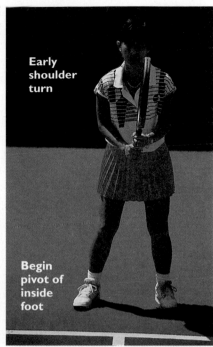

Figure 1.26 Ready position for a groundstroke.

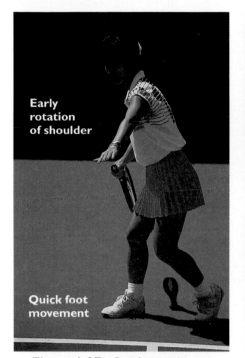

Figure 1.27 Ready position — turn of shoulders (forehand).

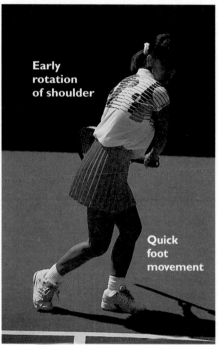

Figure 1.28 Ready position — turn of shoulders (backhand).

LEARNING EXPERIENCE SUGGESTIONS
Ready Position

1. Maintain a base with the feet shoulder width apart.

2. Focus on the ball on the other side of the net.

3. Keep the knees slightly bent and the weight on the balls of the feet.

4. Be relaxed and ready to react.

5. As the ball crosses the net, turn the shoulder and move the feet.

ELIMINATION OF ERRORS (Ready Position)

The Error	What Causes the Error	Correction of the Error
Falling off balance.	Feet too close together.	Widen the base.
Miss-timing the ball.	Not focusing on the ball and not getting shoulders rotated early with feet moving.	Watch the seams of the ball and rotate the shoulders early.

Groundstrokes

2

Groundstrokes are crucial to success in tennis, and they are executed by the player hitting the tennis ball from the baseline area following one bounce of the ball on the court. The groundstroke involves a swinging action designed to hit the ball deep to the opponent's baseline. Both forehand and backhand groundstrokes develop from the basic (little spin) flat stroke and evolve into other groundstrokes termed topspin and slice (underspin) groundstrokes. The two-hand backhand also originates from the basic flat groundstroke, with alterations, giving the two-hand groundstroke its own identity. To accomplish the groundstroke, get in the ready position, and then decide whether to use the forehand or backhand.

GROUNDSTROKES — BASIC FOREHAND

The *basic forehand groundstroke* is the foundation for all forehands hit with spin, and it is the stroke most used by players if they are given the choice between a backhand and a forehand.

The eastern forehand grip — also known as the "shake hands," grip — is used to execute the basic forehand groundstroke.

The basic forehand groundstroke involves three stages — preparing to hit the ball, contacting the ball, and following through. Each stage must be performed in sequence.

Preparing to hit the ball begins with the player in the ready position. Two reactions follow: 1) rotation of the shoulders and 2) movement of the the feet. The racket has to be placed in an early backswing position as a result of

Forehand Groundstroke Loop

Figure 2.1   Pull the racket back in a line even with the eye.

Figure 2.2   Drop the racket below the line of the ball.

Balance A Quarter

Picture an image of balancing a quarter on the edge of your racket to keep the racket perpendicular to the court at contact with the ball.
J. Foster, Tennis, 5/93, p. 28

Racket back

Firm wrist, arm

Figure 2.3   Backswing (eastern forehand grip).

the shoulder and foot movement. To do this, the player may either bring the racket straight back or loop the racket. Either is acceptable, since the goal is to get the racket back in a low position to hit from a semi-low to high position. The loop will be emphasized in this situation as the best method to get the racket back early and in proper position.

The *loop* is broken into two sections: 1) pulling the racket back in a line even with the eye (Figure 2.1), and 2) dropping the racket below the line of the ball at about a twelve-inch position below and behind the intended impact area of the ball (Figure 2.2). The loop will provide a rhythm to the swing, add extra velocity to the ball following impact, and insure a grooved swing.

The full pattern for this *preparation* is to bring the racket back as quickly as possible by reacting early to the ball, and turn the shoulders to begin inertia. As the racket starts back in the loop following the shoulder turn, both feet will move and pivot automatically to accommodate the upper body turn. The racket should move to a perpendicular position to the fence beyond the back court, with the racket slightly higher than the hand and the wrist in a firm position. The arm should be firm, with the elbow slightly bent and away from the body. At the extreme of the backswing position the racket face and the palm will be turned slightly down to the court surface. The final part of the preparation is bending the leg (Figure 2.3).

Contact with the ball begins when the racket moves from the backswing in a semi-low to high pattern. The lead leg steps into the ball with a transfer of weight from back foot to lead foot. The lead leg is bent at contact while the back leg is beginning to straighten. The palm of the hand grasping the racket is behind the ball at impact, with a very firm wrist and with the arm extended eight to ten inches from the body. The non-racket arm is extended toward the ball, giving direction to the ball and balance to the body. The ball is hit off the lead leg at slightly above mid-thigh to waist level. Always step into the ball, transferring your weight forward and keeping the ball away from the body at a position toward the net and sideline (Figure 2.4).

The final part of the sequence is the *follow through*. The wrist remains firm and fixed, and the arm extends out across the body, with the inside of the upper arm touching the chin. The legs lift throughout the follow through, with the lead leg fully extended and the back leg slightly bent. The purpose of the follow through is to eliminate a premature lifting or pulling of the ball before it leaves the racket strings at contact (Figure 2.5).

The *position of the elbow and wrist* and the *transfer of weight* are crucial to the execution of the stroke. It must be emphasized that the wrist and arm remain firm but relaxed throughout the stroke. There is a tendency to lay the wrist back and to hyperextend the elbow. The wrist should not rotate, and the elbow can remain straight or slightly bent. Both should remain firm (Figure 2.6). Weight transfer provides the needed drive behind the ball, with the center of gravity directed forward through the stroke by a stepping motion into the ball. During the weight transfer, the legs must be bent with a change of the degree in bend through the full stroke (Figures 2.7 and 2.8).

Footwork and early preparation are both critical to success with the forehand groundstroke. Footwork supplies the mobility and balance that will provide the base for the stroke, and it sets the stage for weight transfer and leg power. Weight has to be centered over the balls of the feet to effect ease of movement, and the pivoting and lifting actions aid throughout the stroke in placing the body in a position to hit the ball (Figures 2.9 and 2.10). The early preparation includes good shoulder rotation and accompanying foot pivot with a loop backswing. That early response to the opponent's shot is the base for all that follows.

The stroke must be performed in full sequence, with a fluid movement from one part to the next. Any jerky, non-grooved action will detract from the stroke. The acceptable sequence has to include a coordination of feet, legs, shoulder, arm, and wrist. See Figures 2.11–2.13.

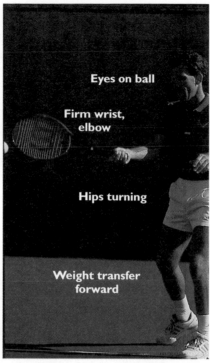

Figure 2.4   Forehand groundstroke contact.

Figure 2.5   Forehand groundstroke follow through.

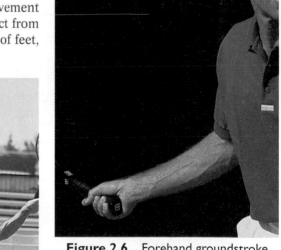

Figure 2.6   Forehand groundstroke closeup of shoulder, elbow, and wrist.

Figure 2.7   Forehand groundstroke contact with transfer of weight.

Figure 2.8   Forehand groundstroke follow through with weight transfer.

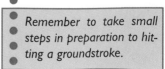

Remember to take small steps in preparation to hitting a groundstroke.

Figure 2.9   Weight to be centered
over the balls of the feet.

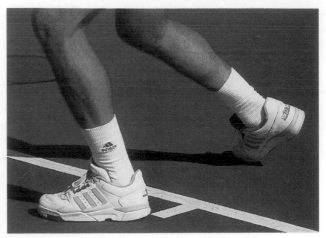

Figure 2.10   Pivoting and lifting actions
aid through the stroke.

Basic Forehand Groundstroke

Figure 2.11   Backswing.

Figure 2.12   Contact.

Figure 2.13   Follow through.

LEARNING EXPERIENCE SUGGESTIONS

Basic Forehand Groundstroke

1. Always start from a ready position.
2. Prepare early with a shoulder rotation and pivot of the feet.
3. Activate the loop backswing or straight back.
4. Step into the ball at contact.

5. Contact the ball with the palm-of-the-hand position and firm wrist.
6. Swing from slightly low to high, with the follow through extending high and across the body.
7. Maintain a full synchronized sequence to the timing of the stroke.

THE ELIMINATION OF ERRORS (Basic Forehand Groundstroke)

The Error	What Causes The Error	Correction of the Error
Ball pulled to the non-racket side of the court.	Hitting too far out in front of the body or pulling the non-racket shoulder.	Step into the ball, hitting off the lead leg. Keep non-racket shoulder tucked into the body.
Ball directed to the near racket side of the court.	Being late in the backswing position, backswing beyond the perpendicular position to the fence, or laying the wrist too far back.	Bring racket back early with a firm wrist and a racket backswing perpendicular in relation to the fence.
Balls hit short with little velocity.	Not stepping into the ball with weight transfer, and poor racket pattern from high to slightly low.	Transfer weight into the ball at contact; change the swinging pattern to slightly low to high.
Balls hit long or high against the opponent's back fence.	Hitting the ball with poor timing, with the weight on the back foot, or in a lifting pattern at contact. Also "breaking wrist" at contact.	Synchronize the timing of the stroke with the slightly low to high racket pattern; use good weight transfer. Keep wrist firm.

FOREHAND GROUNDSTROKE — SLICE AND TOPSPIN

The basic forehand groundstroke is the stroke that beginners start with, but they need to recognize that there is also a *forehand slice groundstroke* and a *forehand topspin groundstroke*. All three strokes are similar, but the slice requires a high backswing and a slightly open face contact point, followed by a high follow through (Figures 2.14–2.16). The spin imparted to the ball is underspin with the ball staying low to the net, followed by a skidding action, or low bounce, when rebounding off the court.

Forehand Slice Groundstroke

Figure 2.14   Backswing (eastern forehand grip).

Figure 2.15   Contact.

Figure 2.16   Follow through.

The topspin stroke begins with a very low backswing, a slightly closed racket face at contact, and a high follow through. At contact there is also some rotation of the forearm. In addition, the legs play a part in this stroke with a low bend of the knees during the backswing, followed by an extension of the legs in the follow-through position (Figures 2.17–2.19). The spin of the ball is an overspin, or top-spin, and the ball action upon striking the court surface is a high bounce. The grip used for a slice is still the eastern forehand grip, but in order to gain additional spin the grip for the topspin changes to a more western grip.

Forehand Topspin Groundstroke

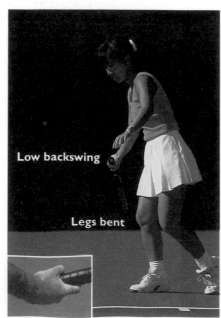

Figure 2.17   Backswing (western forehand grip.

Figure 2.18   Contact.

Figure 2.19   Follow through.

The beginner needs to first develop the basic stroke and move to the slice and topspin in a progression. For most beginners, the slice is more difficult to develop but the forehand topspin groundstroke often comes naturally to many players.

GROUNDSTROKES — BASIC BACKHAND

The basic backhand groundstroke is the easier of the two strokes to hit (i.e., forehand vs. backhand) mechanically, yet it is the stroke that most players fail at in competition. Hitting a backhand is easy and fun, but the player must first develop confidence.

The *grip* used for the basic backhand is the *eastern backhand grip*, with the hand rolled onto the top of the racket grip so that the "V" is pointed to the non-racket shoulder when the racket is held in front of the body. Another guide for the grip is that the knuckles of the racket hand are aligned with the net when the racket makes contact with the ball (Figure 2.20).

As with all forehand strokes and subsequent backhands, there are three phases to the stroke that all mesh into a consistent, grooved feeling. *Preparation in hitting the ball* is based on an early reaction to the ball with an immediate rotation of both shoulders. The feet pivot during the shoulder rotation, and the racket starts its backswing movement with either the loop or straight back technique. The loop is pulled back at eye level and then dropped about eight inches below the contact point of the ball. The swinging pattern is a low-to-high action that is initiated by the backswing in preparation (Figure 2.21).

A change of grips also occurs in the preparation phase. The player begins the stroke from a ready position with an eastern forehand grip. As the player reacts to the ball and turns the shoulders and pivots the feet, the racket begins its backward journey. As the racket moves back, the player uses the non-racket hand to adjust the grip by turning the racket at the throat until the top of the hand is seen as the racket follows the shoulder to the backswing position. The non-racket hand stays in contact with the throat of the racket throughout the backswing and into the movement forward to hit the ball. The racket is perpendicular to the back fence during the final extension backward. The weight of the body is centered over the back foot and the legs are bent, permitting the body to be coiled for the next phase of the stroke.

Contact with the ball occurs with a semi-low-to-high swinging pattern that will insure direction for the ball. The shoulder leads the elbow into the swing, and the elbow leads the wrist. This provides an accumulating effect so that at contact the racket is nearly square to the ball and the joint alignment from shoulder to wrist is a straight line. That joint alignment provides a firm base of support as the ball strikes the racket face. The weight of the body is transferred to the lead leg just prior to contact with the ball, and the position of the racket to the lead leg at contact is mid-thigh to waist level (Figure 2.22).

The *follow through* is an extension of the semi-low-to-high swinging action, with the weight continuing forward off the lead leg as the

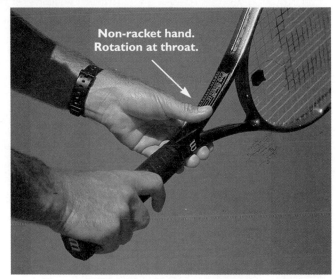

Figure 2.20   Changing grips for the backhand.

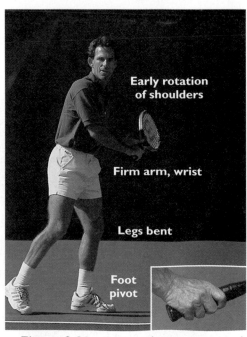

Figure 2.21   Backhand groundstroke preparation (eastern backhand grip).

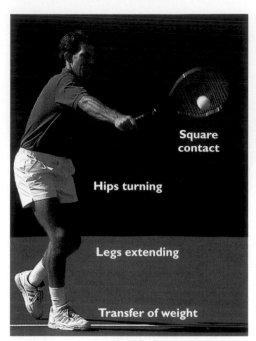

Figure 2.22 Backhand groundstroke contact.

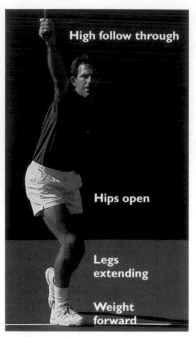

Figure 2.23 Backhand groundstroke follow through.

lead leg straightens and the back leg bends slightly (Figure 2.23). This provides a degree of balance to the base of the stroke. The wrist remains firm as the racket finishes high, facing the racket side of the sideline.

The *wrist, elbow, and shoulder positions* are key elements in the basic backhand groundstroke. The initial shoulder turn followed by the shoulder leading into the stroke are essential in completing the action. The elbow and the wrist should never physically be ahead of the racket (Figure 2.24). The racket should rotate around the wrist, and the wrist should rotate around the elbow from backswing to contact with the ball. At follow through, the racket should lead the wrist and elbow. If the elbow or wrist leads the racket at contact, a pushing action will result, decreasing the velocity of the ball. The racket arm stays closer to the body than with the forehand at a distance of perhaps six to eight inches.

Racket control, weight transfer, footwork, and leg power all contribute to the success or failure of the backhand groundstroke. Racket control is characterized by the loop — pulling the racket back at eye level (Figure 2.25), then dropping the racket below the projected contact point of the ball (Figure 2.26). Balance and weight transfer occur when the player uses proper footwork from the ready position to the final follow through. The critical part of the footwork involves the singular turn of the

Figure 2.24 Backhand groundstroke closeup of shoulder, elbow and wrist.

Figure 2.25 Backhand groundstroke loop — pull the racket back at eye level.

Figure 2.26 Backhand groundstroke loop — drop the racket below the projected contact point of the ball.

non-racket foot when the shoulder rotates (Figure 2.27) and the subsequent stepping into the ball with the racket-side foot just prior to contact with the ball (Figure 2.28). The weight transfer is a total exchange from moving weight from the back foot during preparation to the lead leg at contact on through to follow through (Figures 2.29 and 2.30).

The full sequence of actions involved in the basic backhand groundstroke will determine the outcome of the stroke. There must be a fluid sequence of movement void of all jerky or shaky movement. That sequence should include coordination of shoulders, feet, legs, elbow, and wrist into a mechanically smooth, grooved stroke that causes the racket to make contact with the ball in a nearly square position and that flows to an ultimate follow through (Figures 2.31–2.33). As a final thought, the mechanics of the stroke have to be combined with the belief that the backhand is easier to execute and mechanically more sound than the forehand.

Figure 2.27 Turn the non-racket foot when the shoulder rotates.

Figure 2.28 Step into the ball with the racket-side foot just prior to contact with the ball.

Figure 2.29 Weight should be on the back foot during preparation.

Figure 2.30 Move weight to lead leg at contact through follow through.

Basic Backhand Groundstroke

Figure 2.31 Backswing.

Figure 2.32 Contact.

Figure 2.33 Follow through.

LEARNING EXPERIENCE SUGGESTIONS

Basic Backhand Groundstroke

1. Always start from the ready position.

2. Prepare early with a shoulder rotation and pivot of the feet.

3. Activate the loop backswing or a straight back motion.

4. Change the grip from eastern forehand to eastern backhand as the racket is brought to the backswing position.

5. Keep a firm wrist, and keep the elbow and wrist behind the racket through contact.

6. Transfer the weight from the back foot to the front as the racket moves from backswing to contact to follow through.

7. Contact the ball slightly in front of the lead leg, with the knuckles facing the net at that contact point.

8. Swing low to high, with the racket finishing high and parallel to the racket-side sideline.

9. Keep a full synchronized sequence to the timing of the stroke.

THE ELIMINATION OF ERRORS (Basic Backhand Groundstroke)

The Error	What Causes The Error	Correction of the Error
Ball pulled to the non-racket side of the court.	Hitting too far out in front of the body, or turning the racket shoulder too early.	Step into the ball, hitting off the lead leg. Keep racket shoulder tucked in instead of opening the body.
Ball directed to the non-racket side of the court.	Too late in shoulder turn to initiate a backswing.	Early anticipation and shoulder turn to set up the backswing.
Balls hit short with little velocity.	Not stepping into the ball at contact with minimal weight transfer.	Step into the ball and transfer weight forward. Hit with a flat racket face and follow a racket pattern from semi-low to high.
Balls hit long or high against opponent's fence.	Hitting with poor timing, or weight, on back foot. Also opening racket face too much and not following through.	Synchronize the timing and transfer weight to lead foot at contact and follow through. Make sure to follow through. Also check grip and make sure it is an eastern backhand grip.

Hammer Your Groundstrokes

Think of driving a nail when hitting a groundstroke to give you a firm, powerful stroke that will encourage you to swing through the ball.

K. R. Anderson, *Tennis*, 2/92, p. 26

GROUNDSTROKES — TWO-HAND BACKHAND

The two-hand backhand is immensely popular today with people who need the added strength for force and velocity. The player using the two-hand backhand will gain confidence in the backhand and at the same time sacrifice the reach related to a more conventional stroke. With the exception of the lack of reach, the two-hand backhand provides the opportunity to hit both topspin and slice without changing grips; rather, the change occurs in swing action and in the position of the arms in reference to the body.

In the *two-hand backhand*, the racket-side hand grips the racket with an eastern backhand or continental grip at the butt end of the racket. The non-racket support hand rests on top of the racket-side hand in an eastern forehand grip. The heel of the support hand is nestled snugly between the thumb and index finger of the racket-side hand.

Preparation for hitting the ball involves the basic rotation of the shoulders, except that the rotation will be limited due to the two-hand position. The racket is brought straight back and then dropped low toward the feet. The same foot pivot and weight transfer occur with the two-hand backhand as with other conventional strokes, and the subsequent swing pattern is low to high (Figure 2.34). *Contact with the ball* involves continuation of the low to high pattern with the arms close to the body and the wrists firm. The weight, as with all strokes, is transferred forward to the lead foot as the player steps into the ball to make contact off that lead foot (Figure 2.35). The *follow through* is a simple continuation of the stroke, with the racket finishing wrapped around the non-racket shoulder and head area (Figure 2.36).

> **Swing Like A Batter**
> *Remember to transfer your weight like a batter in baseball would do.*
> J. E. Sever, Tennis, 11/91, p. 27

Basic Two-Hand Backhand Groundstroke

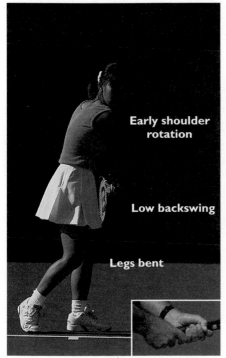

Figure 2.34 Backswing (two-hand backhand grip).

Figure 2.35 Contact.

Figure 2.36 Follow through.

LEARNING EXPERIENCE SUGGESTIONS

Two-Hand Backhand Groundstroke

1. Keep the arms close to the body throughout the stroke and keep the wrists firm.

2. Make sure that the two hands are snug to each other on the grip.

3. Low backswing to wrap around follow through.

THE ELIMINATION OF ERRORS (Two-Hand Backhand Groundstroke)

The Error	What Causes The Error	Correction of the Error
Stroking the ball into the net.	Hitting too far in front of the lead leg or not following the low-to-high pattern.	Hit off the lead leg at contact, or at least follow through high.
Hitting the ball long or high against the fence.	Not dropping the racket to a low position and bending the knees with a low to a high follow through and leg extension.	Swing low to high, and use a low leg bend followed by an extension of the legs.
Hitting the ball off the end of the racket or not getting to the ball in time.	Poor reaction time and little anticipation of where the ball will be hit.	Concentrate on the ball when it is in on the far side of the net. Remember the radius of the reach is shorter with a two-hand backhand than with a one-hand backhand.

BACKHAND GROUNDSTROKE — SLICE AND TOPSPIN

As with the forehand slice and topspin groundstroke it is important to recognize that the basic backhand is the starting point for a beginner, but that there are two additional strokes also known as the *backhand slice groundstroke* and *backhand topspin groundstroke*. The slice is executed with a high backswing, a slightly open racket face at contact, and a high follow through (Figures 2.37–2.40). The ball action is the same underspin with a skidding action as it rebounds from the court.

The topspin groundstroke starts with a low backswing, a slightly closed face at contact, and a high follow through (Figures 2.41–2.44). The forearm does rotate slightly from contact to follow through and the legs bend and extend from backswing to follow through. The eastern backhand grip is used for both the slice and the topspin. A two-hand backhand becomes particularly successful when hitting a topspin backhand since the stroke is compact and already programmed to begin low in the backswing and continue on through to an extensive follow through.

Backhand Groundstroke Slice

Figure 2.37 Backswing.

Figure 2.38 Contact.

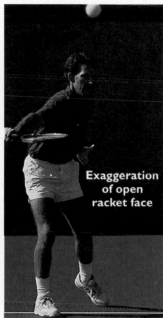

Figure 2.39 Follow through.

Figure 2.40 Follow through.

Backhand Groundstroke Topspin

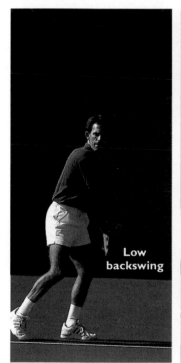

Figure 2.41 Backswing.

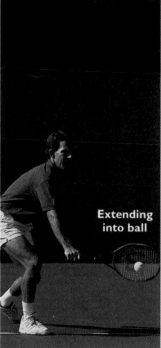

Figure 2.42 Contact.

Figure 2.43 Follow through.

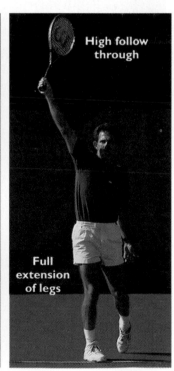

Figure 2.44 Follow through.

Just as with the comments regarding the forehand groundstroke, the beginner needs to start with the basic backhand and progress to spin strokes as development occurs. Often the slice becomes an extremely reliable stroke for the developing player, and the topspin can become quite lethal for a player who develops a two-hand backhand.

SYNOPSIS OF THE USE OF THE GROUNDSTROKE

Groundstrokes are the basis to all play in tennis. The developing player needs to grow with the game and progress from a stationary position of hitting groundstrokes to a moving situation that will allow setting up to hit a ball. The player needs to work on both sides of the body equally so that the forehand and backhand can be developed to balance out the skill aspect of hitting groundstrokes. The beginning player needs to be skilled at simple tasks ranging from dropping a ball and hitting a groundstroke to knowing where home base is, and moving from home base to retrieve and stroke the ball.

Learning how to *drop and hit the ball* to begin a rally is necessary if a player is going to practice, warmup, or actually play the game. In a forehand groundstroke, the drop should be toward the sideline and toward the net so that the player has to extend the arm to reach the ball and step, transferring weight to the lead leg to hit the ball. Dropping the ball anywhere else would confuse the player, eliminate the same form development for each stroke, and provide a difficult set up to begin a rally. One of the reasons for a forehand developing more quickly is that the player practices more on the forehand side. This is because it is more convenient to drop the ball on that side to begin a rally (Figures 2.45 and 2.46).

The drop for the backhand should be attempted as often as the forehand drop to encourage backhand stroke development. The backhand differs from the forehand drop only in that the drop is completed over the top of the racket on the backhand side, and the racket is not yet in a complete backswing position. The ball is dropped in a semi-palm-up position, and a lifting action allows the ball to bounce and come straight back up off the rebound to mid-thigh level to be hit. During the drop and swing, the body is turned to the side, facing the appropriate sideline (Figures 2.47 and 2.48).

Self-Drop For Forehand

Figure 2.45   Drop the ball toward the sideline and toward the net.

Figure 2.46   Ball should bounce and come straight back up to mid-thigh.

Self-Drop For Backhand

Figure 2.47   Drop the ball toward the sideline and toward the net.

Figure 2.48   Ball should bounce and come straight back up to mid-thigh.

All practice with groundstrokes usually begins from a stationary position. The area behind the baseline is known as *home base* (Figure 2.49). It is a great learning experience for the player just beginning to develop the mechanics of a sound groundstroke to have all balls hit deep to that position. The rationale for having balls thrown to students in the early stages of skill development or having a ball machine toss balls directly to a player is to insure that home base is identified and that practice be as consistent as possible. There comes a time, however, when the player has to leave home base and move after a ball hit a distance away. The player must leave the home base area, move toward the ball, and hit a groundstroke — then return to home base.

Moving to the ball, which involves using the proper footwork, is a major problem for the beginning tennis player. If the ball is hit deep with a high and deep bounce, the player must retreat behind the baseline to get to the ball, set up, then step back into the ball with good weight transfer. In order to respond to a deeply hit ball, the player must first turn the shoulder (remember — the player always starts from a ready position) and take a sideward step with the foot that is on the same side as the turning shoulder. From that point, the movement is either a sideward response or a total turn and run to at least a step behind and away from the ball. The turning movement must occur as soon as possible, preferably before the ball crosses the net. See Figure 2.50 (A–E).

Moving to the ball when it is in front of the player is a little easier, but it requires the same anticipation of where the ball is going at as early a time as possible. The player moves in a direct line forward with a timing that will provide opportunity to set up behind the ball and away from the line of the ball's flight. The last part of the movement involves slowing down and gathering the body in a controlled manner, then stepping in a direct line to the ball with the racket side foot first, thus aligning the body to the path of the ball and establishing the next sequential step. The next step involves stepping

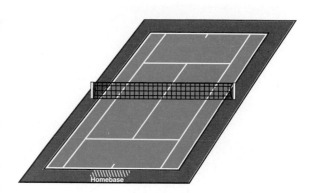

Figure 2.49 Home Base.

Figure 2.50 Footwork and moving to the ball hit beyond the baseline.

Figure 2.51   Footwork and moving to the ball hit
in front of the baseline.

into the ball with the non-racket-side leg in a timed movement to synchronize with the contact part of the full stroke. As the racket-side leg steps first, the racket is in a back-swing position, then it comes through into the ball at contact. See Figures 2.51 (A–D). There is no difference between hitting a forehand or a backhand groundstroke. The point is to set up behind and to the side of the ball as described when dropping the ball to start a rally.

If a *foundation* is built from the base-line that is consistent for all groundstrokes, moving to the ball or hitting from the base-line will be enjoyable. The foundation of hitting with a stepping movement, having good weight transfer, and developing a sound stroke pattern is basic. The foundation must be repeated so often that each stroke is an instinctive reaction not requiring thought.

Moving to hit a ball situated between the baseline and the net is not only related to foot movement, but also to decision making. It is now important to recognize which shots require the player to step into the ball, stroke the ball, then return to home base, or to move up to the ball and hit it followed by an advancement to the net. Shots that are hit at the service court line require the decision to continue the advance to the net to play a potential volley, or to retreat back to home base. Balls that are hit between the service court line and the net require no decision — the player is forced to move forward to play at the net (Figure 2.52). When a decision must be made to either attack the net or retreat to the baseline, or when the player must go to the net, a modification of the groundstroke, called an *approach shot*, has been enacted.

When it is determined that the player is going to hit an approach shot, there are certain perceptions that the player must develop. First, the player must realize that the approach shot is simply a groundstroke that must be moved toward in order for the ball to be hit. Second, the approach must be viewed as a gift given as a reward for excellent play on the base-line that forced the opponent to hit the ball short rather than deep. Third, the player must recognize that approach shots often give the player too much time to decide what to do with the ball, resulting in a shabby attempt at hitting an approach shot. Fourth, the approach shot must be considered a modified version of the full groundstroke swing.

The third and fourth concepts need to be discussed in more detail. Being given too much time to hit a shot allows the

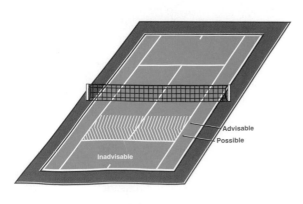

Figure 2.52   Foundation — when to go to the net,
when to stay at home base.

player to decide how and where to hit the ball. However, a problem exists when the player changes the decision once it has been made. The player must make one decision on how to hit the ball, and another on where to hit the ball (i.e., deep or at an angle). Both judgments are difficult for beginning players, and as a result, they simply bang away at the ball, usually missing everything but the back fence. The player must be aware of the choices and continue to learn from mistakes, gaining confidence from each opportunity to hit an approach shot (Figure 2.53).

Modifying the approach shot to cope with the close target area is the skill adaptation to the groundstroke. There are three adaptations to the approach shot from the groundstroke: 1) shorten the backswing, 2) visualize the target, and 3) select the appropriate shot sequence. An approach shot doesn't need extensive force behind it as does a shot from the baseline. Instead of bringing the racket back perpendicular to the back fence, it can be brought back perhaps two-thirds of that distance. If the player will develop a mental imagery of the target as being located at the opponent's service court line, the ensuing distance traveled by the ball will probably be increased by a third of the distance. As a result, the ball will really travel to the opponent's baseline. The baseline is the spot desired for a deep hit, but the mental imagery has to give a short target distance to allow for the short distance that the ball must actually travel. Selecting the appropriate shot is based on the position of the ball to be hit. Balls that are returned low are usually hit to the backhand of the opponent, with the player then moving to the net to hit a volley off the opponent's assumed weaker backhand return. Returns that hit the center of the court have a target area of the corners. Hitting a ball cross court that is positioned down the line opens up too much court for a successful return by the opposing player.

The sequence of moving from the baseline to hitting an approach shot is continued by the player moving on to the net to play a potential volley return of the opponent's reaction to the approach shot. The description of the volley sequence is found in the following chapter.

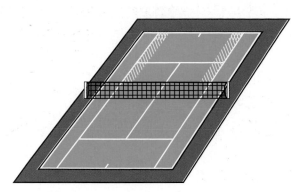

Figure 2.53 Approach shots down the line and in the corners.

Net Play

The volley is one of two strokes hit when the ball is in mid-air prior to striking the court on the bounce. It is an uncomplicated punching action stroke that is also described as a "blocking the ball action." The volley is used in singles play following an approach shot or in a serve and volley combination. In doubles, the volley also is used following an approach shot and as a serve and volley combination, and it is used with a player positioned at the net during a serve. All players must learn the skills involved in the volley early in their development. A singles player may avoid most situations involving the volley, but in doubles play there is no choice but to be located at the net on nearly every shot played.

The volley shot begins from the *ready position* for the groundstroke except that the racket is held higher at chin level. From this position, the player may respond to either a forehand or backhand volley while located at the net. Part of the preparation in the ready position is to assume a grip that is both comfortable and functional. The *continental grip* is usually recommended for the volley, since no adjustment must be made for a forehand or a backhand volley (Figure 3.1). Often there is not enough time to change grips when at the net due to the high velocity of a ball and the short distance from the opposing player. The strength of the continental grip is that the backhand is firm and solid when punching the volley. The weakness is that the grip for a forehand provides a weaker base, forcing the player to adjust at the net by changing to an eastern forehand when time

Figure 3.1 Volley ready position (continental grip).

29

permits. Most successful players, in fact, do "cheat" and move the hand on the grip for most volley shots providing that they have the time to not only change, but to also change back following the stroke.

The *forehand volley* begins with a "short" backswing caused by a shoulder turn. The racket head is located above the hand as the racket is taken back only even with the racket shoulder (Figure 3.2). The *preparation* is completed with the weight centered on the racket-side foot. The racket comes forward at *contact* with the ball, with the face of the racket striking the back of the ball squarely at the front of the lead leg (Figure 3.3). A slight downward path of the stroke imparts some underspin to the ball. At contact, the racket head is above the hand, the wrist is very firm, and the grip is tight to prevent the racket from turning in the hand at impact. A step is also taken with the opposing leg, and the weight is transferred to that leg. The knees are bent from backswing to contact. It should be repeated that the racket must be in front of the lead leg at contact. The *follow through* (Figure 3.4) is the final part of the punching action. A short downward motion, with the bottom edge of the racket leading, completes the stroke. The lead leg is still bent during follow through, with the weight centered over that leg. Upon completion of follow through, the player must return to a ready position in preparation for the next volley.

Be a Tiger

Be a tiger at the net and pounce on the volley by being active and aggressive.

J. DeAndrade, Tennis, 4/93, p. 38

Forehand Volley Sequence

Figure 3.2 Preparation.

Figure 3.3 Contact with the ball.

Figure 3.4 Follow through.

Be a Fencer

Play the net like a fencer. Step into the volley with a lunge and attack the ball.

G. H. Tanelli, Tennis, 3/93, p. 12

The *backhand volley* is executed like the forehand volley, but it is easier to mechanically complete since the shoulder turn is already to the backhand side and the elbow and shoulder work as a firm backboard when striking the ball. In *preparation*, the racket head is brought back to the non-racket side and is positioned above the hand. The weight of the body is centered over the non-racket-side foot, and the backswing is short with a firm wrist. At *contact*, the weight is shifted forward to the racket leg as that leg steps into the ball (Figure 3.5). The racket face strings make full square contact with the back of the ball with a punching action that includes a firm wrist and arm and a tight grip on the racket. Contact is made slightly in front of the lead leg, with the racket above the hand (Figure 3.6). The knees are bent from preparation through contact and into the follow through. The *follow through* is a continuation of the punch action, with the bottom edge of the racket leading to apply a small degree of spin to the ball (Figure 3.7). At the end of the follow through, the weight is centered on the leading leg, and the racket is extended a short distance forward. The recovery must be quick as the player returns to the ready position at the net.

Backhand Volley Sequence

Figure 3.5 Preparation.

Figure 3.6 Contact with the ball.

Figure 3.7 Follow through.

LEARNING EXPERIENCE SUGGESTIONS
Volley

1. Punch the ball — do not swing at it.
2. Backswing and follow through are short.
3. Keep the racket above the hand throughout the stroke.
4. Step into the ball if there is time.
5. Stay low on the ball.
6. Hit behind the ball, then follow through with the bottom edge of the racket leading.
7. Make contact in front of the lead leg.
8. Begin with the continental grip, but "cheat" when there is time.
9. Maintain control of the racket with a firm grip and firm wrist throughout the stroke.

THE ELIMINATION OF ERRORS (Volley)

The Error	What Causes The Error	Correction of the Error
Balls that have no pace or just drop off the racket strings.	Not hitting in front of the lead leg. Not transferring weight into the ball at contact.	Hit slightly in front of the lead leg between the body and net. Step into the ball.
Racket turns in the hand, causing lack of control of the ball.	Lack of a firm grip, or grip size is too small.	Tighten the grip or increase the size of the grip for better control.
The ball strikes the net following contact.	Player did not get "down" on the ball and bend the knees. Ball may be below height of net.	Bend the knees all the way through the shot. Open racket face if ball is below height of net.
Ball pushes the racket back at contact.	Elbow and arm are not providing a firm backboard.	Align the wrist, arm, and shoulder in a firm position.

Anticipation is a key to playing well at the net. If the player at the net is afraid of the ball, there will be no anticipation. If the player "sees" the ball early, reacting as the ball comes off the opposing player's racket rather than waiting until the ball arrives at the net, the volleying player will be effective at the net. Once the reaction has been improved, the next important phase is to attack by stepping into the ball rather than waiting for the ball to arrive at the net. Even guessing, as part of anticipation, is better than standing at the net and waiting.

Footwork for the volley is an important aspect of the stroke so that form can be added to the total maneuver. Footwork enables the player to step into the ball with body weight behind the punch, and to move efficiently to get to the ball. The first part of the footwork involves a shoulder turn and hip pivot. From a ready position, the player should pivot the hips toward the anticipated position of the ball. With the hip turn, the shoulders will also turn, and the racket side foot will react by pivoting until the body weight centers over that foot.

There are three basic ball positions presented to the volleyer: 1) the setup with the shoulder and hip turn, involving a small cross-step, 2) the wide ball that forces the player to take a lengthened cross-step, and 3) the ball hit at the player that requires a defensive reaction. The *setup* is initiated with the shoulder and hip turn, followed by the turn of the inside of the foot and a step forward and a little across the body with the opposite leg (Figures 3.8 and 3.9). The *wide ball* is reached by the same movement used

Figure 3.8 Footwork for the setup volley (forehand).

Figure 3.9 Footwork for the setup volley (backhand).

for the setup, but the step across the body with the opposite leg requires an elongated, direct movement. See Figures 3.10 and 3.11.

The *ball hit at the player* requires that the player hit with a backhand volley, if at all possible. The player must pivot off the racket foot and step with the non-racket foot behind the opposite foot to turn the shoulder sideways to the ball. The player must then lean back into the path of the ball (Figure 3.12).

Body elevation is also important to successful completion of the volley, since balls are not going to be returned at shoulder level in

Figure 3.10 Footwork for the wide ball volley (forehand).

Figure 3.11 Footwork for the wide ball volley (backhand).

all situations. The legs must be either bent or extended for many of the volley stroke situations.

A *low volley* forces the player to bend the knees and get low to the ball (Figures 3.13 and 3.14). The hip and shoulder turn must occur to position the shoulder to the ball, and the legs must bend as low as possible. The volleyer steps into the ball with the opposite foot and punches under and through the ball, using underspin to lift the ball over the net. The underspin is achieved by opening the racket face. The closer the ball is to the court at contact, the more open the racket face should be. The follow through of the low shot continues with an upward, short movement of the racket, with the knees remaining bent. Throughout the stroke, the racket should stay above the hand, if possible, to insure proper technique and stroking action.

The *high volley* forces the volleyer to extend the body and the legs to reach the ball. The shoulder turn must occur early to permit the racket to be taken back a little further and higher than for the basic volley. The

Figure 3.12 Footwork for the ball hit at the net player (backhand).

Figure 3.13 Low forehand volley.

Bend knees

Open racket face

Figure 3.14 Low backhand volley.

Bend knees   Open racket face

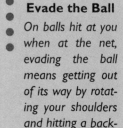

Evade the Ball

On balls hit at you when at the net, evading the ball means getting out of its way by rotating your shoulders and hitting a backhand volley.

D. Van Der Meer, *Tennis*, 4/92, p. 89

Figure 3.15   High forehand volley.

Figure 3.16   High backhand volley.

player then steps into the ball with the opposite leg and punches down and through the ball. The follow through moves in the direction of the ball just hit and ends at waist level. The punching pattern is a high-to-low closing stroke. The wrist is locked and the stroke is firm. See Figures 3.15 and 3.16)

The volley needs to be *incorporated into the total game* of the beginning player. At this point, the volley is an extension of the player hitting a groundstroke and advancing to the net, or hitting an approach shot and moving to the net, or hitting at the net in a doubles play situation. The volley is a reward for forcing the opponent into a mistake, and it is executed best between the service court line and the net. The beginning player will play most volleys off the net at a range of one to one and one-half racket lengths away from the net. The more advanced player has an increased range back to the service court line, but that same player has the goal of moving closer to the net to be less vulnerable to a well-placed low shot at the feet.

Half-volleys are necessary when the player is positioned in the midcourt area and is confronted with a return shot placed just in front of the feet. The player uses an eastern forehand or backhand grip, or a continental grip, and strokes the ball as a combination groundstroke and volley. The player must bend both legs to the extreme, with the lead leg bent at a right angle and the back leg nearly scraping the court surface. The ball must be contacted on the "short" bounce or before it rises. The wrist is firm at contact, and the angle of the racket face is open just enough to permit the ball to clear the net. The backswing is short, as with an approach shot, and the follow through lifts the body up from the low position. Throughout the shot, the head should stay down to insure that the body does not lift early. The forehand half-volley contact point is at the lead leg, and the backhand point is in front of the lead leg. See Figures 3.17 and 3.18.

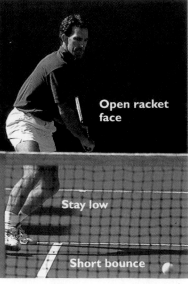

Figure 3.17   Forehand half-volley.

Figure 3.18   Backhand half-volley.

The Service and Service Return

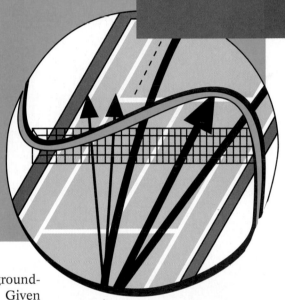

The service and service return are critical to success in tennis. A groundstroke skill enables the developing player to rally from the baseline. Given the skills of approach shots and the volley, the player can attack the opposing player. Without the skills of service and service return, the beginning player is not able to place the ball into play for an actual game, set, or match, or be able to return a service. The three services that are widely used in tennis are: 1) the basic flat service, 2) the slice service, and 3) the topspin service. Discussion will be limited to the first two serves.

THE BASIC FLAT SERVICE

The *basic flat service* is a model for the service. A *service stance* is used in all serves. The feet are approximately shoulder width apart, with the lead foot positioned approximately the length of a tennis ball from the baseline and the center mark of the baseline. The shoulder is pointed toward the service court target, the knees are slightly flexed, and the body from the waist up is upright (Figure 4.1).

The *grip* for the *flat service* (and for the two other services) is the continental, with some possible slight variations. The continental grip provides a flat surface for a square contact point. When learning to serve, you may begin by using an eastern forehand or western forehand grip, but you should change to a continental grip as soon as possible.

Figure 4.1 Service stance (continental grip).

A skill is involved in *holding the ball for the toss* that initiates the serve action and also *in the actual tossing of the ball*. To begin any service, you must have two tennis balls in your possession. Keep one ball in the pocket of your tennis shorts so that only one ball needs to be coped with during any one serve. The ball to be tossed should be grasped with the fingertips and the thumb, with the heel of the hand pointing in the direction of the toss (Figure 4.2). From the support base, the ball is placed into a position off the lead shoulder between the player and the sideline, and higher than the reach of the racket. A straight arm lifts the ball from the waist to above the head. The heel of the hand is raised during the full arm movement. As the tossing arm begins the upward movement, the racket arm brings the racket back in a synchronization with the toss. At the extension of the arm reach, the ball is released, culminating the lifting action. The toss must be executed the same way over and over again so that you become consistent (Figures 4.3 and 4.4).

Figure 4.2 Beginning of toss.

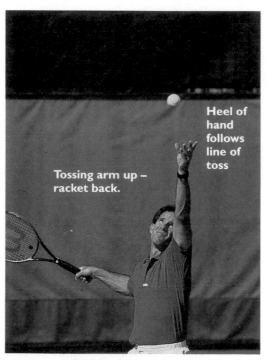

Figure 4.3 Release.

Figure 4.4 Height of toss.

When first learning the service, keep the feet shoulder width apart throughout the serve. Initially, stability is more important than extra rhythm. Although the feet will not come together in the early stages of learning, the back foot will come forward as the weight transfers toward the target on the follow through (Figures 4.5–4.7).

The first timing aspect of the service is the *toss synchronization as the preparation for the service*. As the tossing hand begins the upward lift of the ball, the racket begins a backward movement with the arm straight. The two arms move in opposition. The racket continues back, with the elbow bending as the racket approaches the shoulder blade area. The back of the elbow is at a right angle, and the arm is in an overhand throwing position. As the ball reaches the top of the placement and begins to fall, the tossing hand will drop away, and the hitting elbow will stay in a right-angle position. See Figures 4.8–4.12.

The beginning of *contact from the half-service position* now occurs. The legs straighten from a bent position in preparation to bringing the racket through in a striking position, with the wrist and forearm breaking through

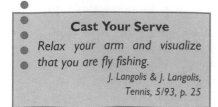

Cast Your Serve

Relax your arm and visualize that you are fly fishing.

J. Langolis & J. Langolis,
Tennis, 5/93, p. 25

Footwork For Service

Figure 4.5 Backswing.   **Figure 4.6** Contact.   **Figure 4.7** Follow through.

the ball. The arm and body are fully stretched. The back and top of the ball is hit with the racket face at about four inches down from the height of the toss. The body, led by the shoulder, opens up to the position of the ball at contact (Figure 4.13).

The follow through continues as momentum carries the racket through the ball and on down to the far non-racket-side leg. A definite weight transfer occurs during follow through, with the momentum of the racket side pulling the body down and forward. This forces the back foot at the last moment to step forward for a balanced finish (Figures 4.14–4.16).

The basic flat service is designed mechanically to hit through and down on the ball. The ball cannot be hit directly down in a straight line unless the server is at least 6'7" tall. The racket makes an upward movement at contact followed by a breaking of the wrist and forearm through the ball. Most beginning players have a great desire to hit the flat serve as hard as they can, assuming that the idea is to hit the service with blazing speed. The problem with such a view is that few balls are placed accurately into the appropriate service court, which, in turn, means that the ball hasn't been placed in play to begin a point. The fun of playing the game is decreased and the possibility for success is minimized by first serves that miss the target. The idea is to hit a firm, controlled, rhythmical service that is placed in the service court effectively. Rhythm and ball placement are far more effective than a sometimes accurate, high-velocity serve.

The *execution of a full versus a half-service* requires discussion. Some beginning instruction starts the player with the racket already positioned between the shoulder blades to eliminate the initial take-back portion of the stroke preparation. The purpose is to keep the stroke as simple as possible and not complicate the coordination of the stroke. The choice of a full versus a half-serve is a simple one of efficiency. Some highly skilled players use a half-service position, where many less-skilled players use a full service. Some players are more comfortable initially with a full-service sequence, but all players need to see the half-service position to understand the upward position of the elbow and the location of the racket during the backswing to permit accurate timing of the stroke. Refer to Figures 4.8–4.16 on the following pages.

Flat Service

Figure 4.8   Beginning of toss.

Figure 4.9   Release of ball and take back of racket.

Figure 4.10   Backswing continuation in preparation sequence.

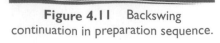

Figure 4.11   Backswing continuation in preparation sequence.

Figure 4.12   Full backswing preparation sequence.

Figure 4.13   At contact.

Flat Service (continued)

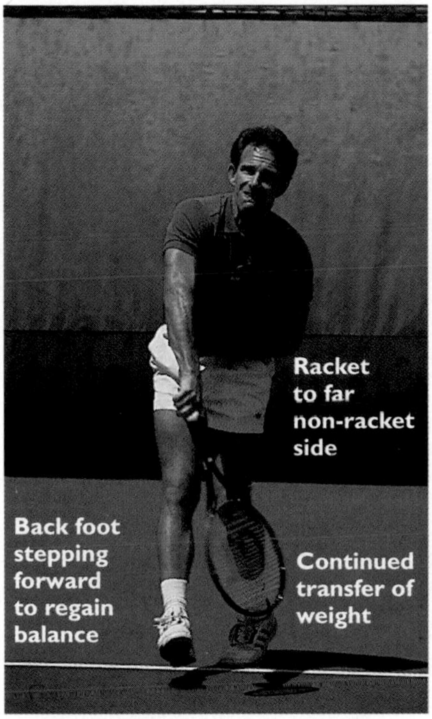

Figure 4.14 Follow through sequence.

Figure 4.15 Follow through sequence.

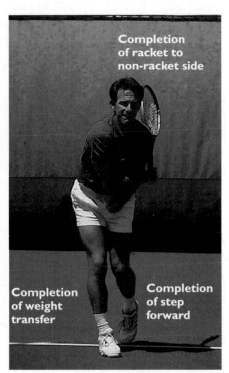

Figure 4.16 Completion of follow through sequence.

LEARNING EXPERIENCE SUGGESTIONS

Basic Flat Serve

1. Use the continental grip as soon as possible.

2. Time the toss with the take-back of the racket.

3. Keep the tossing arm straight, with the heel of the hand lifting in the direction of the toss.

4. The toss should be higher than the racket can reach.

5. Release the ball at the extension of the arm.

6. Keep the elbow up and at a right angle at the extension of the backswing.

7. Coil the body by arching the back and bending the knees during preparation.

8. Bring the racket through the ball with a slight upward, followed by a downward, wrist and forearm break.

9. Let the weight transfer carry the body and racket forward in the direction of the ball, with the back foot coming forward to regain balance.

10. Make sure that the racket follows on through to the non-racket-side hip.

THE ELIMINATION OF ERRORS (Basic Flat Serve)

The Error	What Causes The Error	Correction of the Error
Erratic placement of the serve.	Inconsistent toss.	Toss the ball by laying it off the lead shoulder between the shoulder and the sideline at a height above the reach of the racket.
Balls served short.	The ball is either hit too far out in front of the server toward the net; the server attempts to hit over the ball or the ball is too low at contact.	Again, the toss must be off the lead shoulder, placed at a height above the reach of the racket and between the server and the sideline.
Ball toss goes behind the head.	Not lifting in a straight line with the tossing arm.	Use the heel of the hand as the lifting agent giving direction to the ball.
Ball served long.	Racket under the ball at contact, pushing the ball up; trying to hit the ball too hard.	The toss must be off the lead shoulder; placed at a height above the reach of the racket and between the server and and sideline. Slow racket head speed.
Stepping on the baseline during the serve.	Toss is too far over the baseline toward the net or the player steps with the foot as if throwing a ball.	Toss the ball by laying it off the lead shoulder between the shoulder and the sideline at a height above the reach of the racket. The player needs to glue the lead foot to the court.

THE SLICE SERVICE

The slice service involves a side spin, and it is usually used as a second serve in singles and a first and second serve in doubles. The spin permits the server to hit with greater accuracy and still hit a deep placement of serve. A side spin is imparted by contacting the back and side of the ball. The result is that the ball lands in the court and kicks away from the position of the server.

The *slice service differs from the flat service* in the toss position and in the movement pattern of the racket. The toss is the same distance from the body, but with less height (one of the advantages in the wind is a lower toss for a slice service). The ball is tossed between the lead shoulder and the middle of the body. More spin and less velocity is achieved the closer the toss is to the back of the racket shoulder. The difference between the slice and flat serve toss is that the flat serve toss is above the reach of the racket as compared to the shorter toss for a slice service, and the toss is off the lead shoulder instead of between the lead shoulder and the middle of the body. See Figures 4.17–4.20 for comparison. During a slice service, contact is made on the side and back of the ball just below center, with the racket moving from high to low. The wrist and forearm snaps at contact with a controlled, firm movement. The shoulders are turned more with a slice service, leaving the body even more open at contact than with the flat service. That openness is due to a small change in foot position, with the back foot placed slightly behind the lead foot (Figures 4.21–4.24).

Toss for Flat Serve

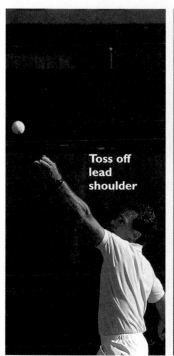

Figure 4.17 Toss is off the lead shoulder.

Figure 4.18 Toss should be above the reach of the racket.

Toss for Slice Serve

Figure 4.19 Toss between the lead shoulder and middle of the body.

Figure 4.20 Toss should not be above the reach of the racket.

Figure 4.21 Flat service contact.

Figure 4.22 Slice service contact.

Figure 4.23 Flat service foot position.

Figure 4.24 Slice service foot position.

The *full sequence of the slice service,* including the exceptions identified above, is a rhythmical service with the take away, followed by the contact with the ball, and culminating with a follow through down off the hip of the non-racket side. The weight transfer is an aid to that sequence, as is the leg bend followed by the extension of the leg at contact (Figures 4.25–4.28).

A *summary of the differences and commonalities* of the two services may be helpful to the developing player. The differences are related to ball toss position, racket pattern movement, and foot position on the baseline and are outlined in Table 4.1. The commonalities involve weight transfer, elbow position on the backswing, and follow through off the non-racket-side hip. One additional commonality that will enhance the rhythm and timing of the total stroke is a change in foot movement from preparation through contact for the developing player. Instead of maintaining stability with a stationary foot position, the developing player may bring the back foot up even with the lead foot as the racket pattern begins to close on the ball at contact. This small change should be utilized when the player has developed balance and stroke timing from a more stationary position.

Slice Service

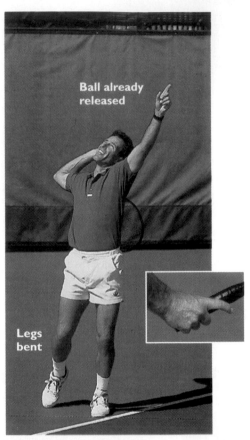

Figure 4.25 Backswing (continental grip).

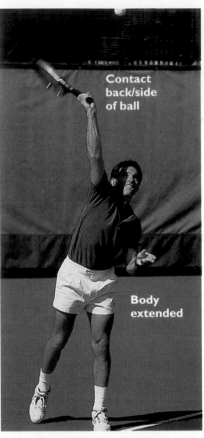

Figure 4.26 Contact.

Figure 4.27 Follow through.

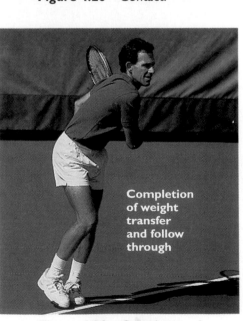

Figure 4.28 Completion of follow through.

TYPE OF SERVICE	BALL TOSS PLACEMENT	FOOT POSITION ON BASELINE	RACKET PATTERN MOVEMENT	CONTACT POSITION ON BALL
Flat	off lead shoulder, above racket reach	even	straight through	back-top
Slice	between lead shoulder and racket shoulder, lower than racket reach	back foot slightly back	curving line	back-side under center

TABLE 4.1 ● Differences Between the Two Major Services

LEARNING EXPERIENCE SUGGESTIONS

Slice Serve

1. Toss the ball lower than on the flat service, and toss more toward the back shoulder to obtain more spin.
2. Contact the ball on the back and side below center.
3. Open the serving stance more than with the flat service.
4. Use a continental grip.
5. Transfer weight forward through the sequence of the service, allowing the back foot to move forward to regain balance after contact.

THE ELIMINATION OF ERRORS (Slice Serve)

The Error	What Causes The Error	Correction of the Error
Lack of spin on the ball.	Toss not far enough back to the racket shoulder; no continental grip; body doesn't open to the ball.	Toss between the two shoulders, check to make sure the grip is continental, or turn the lead shoulder more through the stroke.
Pulling the ball out of the serving court.	Turning the non-racket shoulder into the ball too early, and pulling the shoulder too far through the ball.	Point the non-racket shoulder to the service court target area from contact through follow through.
A great amount of spin, but little velocity or distance.	Ball is hit too far back on back shoulder, or racket pattern is too far to the outside of the ball at contact.	Move toss toward the lead shoulder and/or control racket pattern to the backside under center spot on the ball.
Hitting the ball off the racket edge.	Too much of an eastern backhand grip.	Use a continental grip.

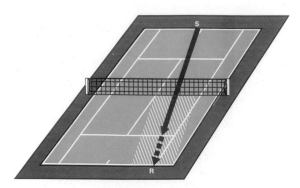

Figure 4.29   Return of serve position.

Figure 4.30   Return of serve
ready position.

THE RETURN
OF SERVICE

Because there are different services with different velocities, trajectories, and spins, the beginning player may be confronted with a series of decisions related to coping with each type of serve.

Return of serve positioning is a matter of mathematics. The receiver must split the court in half in a line from the server to the receiver (Figure 4.29). The receiver cannot overplay to the side, attempting to return all serves with a forehand, since a server with an adequate slice serve can place a ball that will kick off the court and out of the reach of the player favoring the side. It is much better for the receiver to position with the potential to hit either a forehand or backhand equally. The depth of the receiver's position depends on the strength of the server and the velocity of the ball. If a player pushes the ball when serving and simply gets the ball in play, the receiver can move up and stand inside the baseline about halfway between the baseline and the service court line. If the server has a strong serve with high velocity, the receiver should stand at or slightly behind the baseline.

Returning the served ball effectively requires a special set of skills. First, the receiver should develop a relaxed attitude and physical position. The ready position (Figure 4.30), as a second check, should be high to permit quick lateral movement and enable the receiver to hit through the ball with a minimal amount of adjustment. The third reaction is for the receiver to rotate the shoulders to a hitting position at the earliest possible moment. Fourth, the receiver must transfer weight into the stroke by stepping into the ball at contact. A fifth consideration is for the player to adopt a volley concept to the stroke. The backswing and follow through need to be shortened to a movement longer than a volley but shorter than a groundstroke. The short-ened backswing enables the receiver to control the racket and bring it through in time to contact the ball. The action of the racket is a blocking or punching movement that pushes the ball back across the net, reversing the velocity of the serve. The racket should be square to the ball and a little out in front of the lead leg, with a short follow through to add direction to the ball. Sixth, the racket should be held firmly throughout the stroke, and particularly at contact. Finally, the receiver must watch the ball as long as possible up to the point of contact. Return of serve follows the same process and skill pattern whether hitting a forehand (Figures 4.31–4.34) or backhand (Figures 4.35–4.38). The key to selection of the side to hit from depends on the spin and direction of the ball and a responsive early rotation of the shoulders based on anticipation of the position of the ball.

Target for return of serve is a moot point if the return player is just trying to get the racket on the ball. But with a degree of skill at returning a serve, the receiver can return the ball to spots on the court. The first consideration is where *not* to place the ball. Balls hit short to the server are a reward to that server, so it is important to eliminate short returns. Serves that pull a return player off the court should be returned down the sideline rather than cross-court, and most returns hit soft and "up" should be avoided. If the receiver can remember to return deep with pace and velocity on the ball, subsequent play should enable the receiver to gain equal footing in a baseline rally.

Anticipation of the serve is both a physical and mental phase of return of service. The receiver must look at the body language of the server and concentrate on the ball. The body language will provide clues to the spin and

Return of Serve — Forehand

Figure 4.31 Backswing.

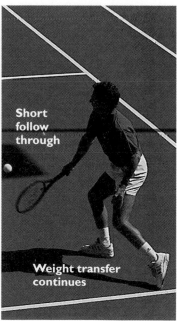

Figure 4.32 Contact.

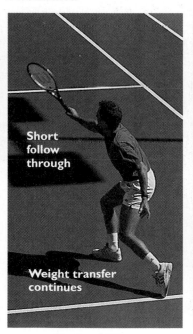

Figure 4.33 Follow through.

Figure 4.34 Completion of follow through.

Return of Serve — Backhand

Figure 4.35 Backswing.

Figure 4.36 Contact.

Figure 4.37 Follow through.

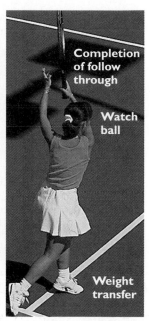

Figure 4.38 Completion of follow through.

velocity of the ball. If the racket face pattern is to the outside of the ball and the toss is short and back toward the racket shoulder, the serve will be a slice. If the toss is off the lead shoulder and toward the net, the ball will be a flat serve. A topspin serve will be interpreted by a toss above the head and/or more back arch than usual. Velocity of the ball can be observed to some extent by the effort made by the server. Concentration on the seams of the ball will permit the receiver to physically react to the direction of the ball. The mental efforts all combine to allow the receiver to make an early shoulder turn and pivot of the feet, thus placing the racket in a backswing position.

LEARNING EXPERIENCE SUGGESTIONS

Return of Serve

1. Be relaxed when waiting to return a serve.
2. Concentrate on the server's body language and on the ball throughout the serve.
3. Get the racket back early.
4. Be aggressive and step into the ball at contact.
5. Use a compact swing with a short backswing and follow through.
6. Maintain a firm grip on the racket at contact.

7. Hit deep on all serves, and hit with a ground-stroke swing on soft serves that are deep to the receiver's service court.
8. Soft and short serves should be returned with an approach shot concept.
9. Block all high-velocity serves, and block deep and to the baseline.
10. Return every serve by placing the racket on the ball on every service.

THE ELIMINATION OF ERRORS (Return of Serve)

The Error	What Causes The Error	Correction of the Error
Hitting the ball out beyond the server's baseline.	Swinging with a full groundstroke swing.	Use a compact swing, block high velocity serves.
Pulling the ball across the court to the sidelines.	Ahead of the arrival of the ball with the racket.	Judge the velocity of the ball, and time the swing.
Ball coming off the racket late with direction toward the near sideline.	Not anticipating early, and as a result, not getting the shoulders turned and the racket back early.	Watch the ball, and communicate mental observation to the physical reaction of turning the shoulders and pivoting the feet.
Cannot control direction of the ball.	Wrist isn't firm and grip isn't tight.	Keep a firm wrist and grip at contact.

The Aerial Game

The lob and overhead smash combinations are basic strokes for the beginning player. Each skill compliments the other in tennis. The lob is an extension of the groundstroke discussed in Chapter 2, and the overhead smash is an elaboration of the service discussed in the preceding chapter. Each is part of the transition package for the beginning learner moving to a more advanced level of play.

THE OVERHEAD SMASH

The basic forehand overhead smash is a flat serve from the half-swing position. The overhead is hit from either the forehand or backhand side, but most players run around the backhand to play a forehand overhead. There are two overhead smashes in tennis — the simplistic orthodox overhead with little foot movement and a simple swing, and the more complex overhead characterized by additional agility and timing (Figure 5.1). The orthodox overhead smash is the only smash to be discussed below. The eastern forehand or continental grip is used for all forehand overheads.

The *orthodox forehand overhead smash* as a forehand is a simple transition from the flat service. The player must maneuver underneath the ball that is hit as a lob, and from that position bring the racket back to the middle of the shoulder blades with the racket elbow at a right angle. The position of the racket physically touching between the shoulder blades provides a reference point for the player hitting the overhead. The reaction that occurs simultaneously with the racket moving to a ready position is for the player to point with the non-racket arm and hand to the ball as a second reference

Figure 5.1 Complex overhead smash.

Figure 5.2 Orthodox overhead smash ready position (eastern forehand or continental grip).

point. The line of the flight of the ball is similar to the ball toss, but the ball falls at a more rapid speed and at a slightly different angle. The feet are shoulder width apart, and the non-racket shoulder has turned to face the net and the intended target area (Figure 5.2).

In executing the overhead, the body of the player is coiled and gathered, ready to time the stroke. The ball is hit off the lead shoulder, with the legs extending and the body uncoiling. Contact of the racket to ball involves an up and over motion, providing a little topspin for greater net clearance and depth. The racket comes through the ball with a wrist break and a follow through to the far hip, but the action is shortened to accommodate the return of a ready position for the next shot (Figures 5.3–5.6).

The full stroke is simplistic, eliminating wasted motion and extraneous actions. The feet remain where they were until the follow through pulls the back foot forward to catch the balance of the player at the completion of the follow through. The player is encouraged to hit out on the ball with smooth, rhythmical timing and control.

Advancing to more agility with the forehand overhead smash involves adding a few parts to the stroke. First, it is important to set up to hit the overhead. That movement consists of long running strides to get to the general area as fast as possible so that the stroke can be set up with adequate time. Once in the general area, the player will be situated behind the anticipated drop of the ball. At this point, the player takes small steps to adjust to the position of the ball. Balls that are hit over the player's head are handled in the same manner — taking long strides to get behind the ball, then short steps to adjust to the falling pattern of the ball.

Bouncing the overhead means permitting the ball to bounce before executing an overhead smash. There are two situations in which the lob is

Orthodox Forehand Overhead Smash

Figure 5.3 Preparation.

Figure 5.4 Contact.

Figure 5.5 Wrist break. Follow through.

Figure 5.6 Completion of follow through.

allowed to bounce prior to being hit as an overhead smash. Lobs that have a very high loft are permitted to bounce so that a better timing can occur when hitting the overhead. Lobs that are short at the net, eliminating a good set position for the overhead, are also usually allowed to bounce. Hitting a high lob following a bounce is similar to hitting the overhead from a mid-air position following a lob. The additional time that is generated when permitting a bounce gives the opponent an opportunity to recover, and it gives the player hitting the overhead a chance to place the ball more effectively. When hitting a lob that bounces short, you need to remember to stay low enough so that the stroke is still angled down and through the ball. The goal for the overhead return of a short ball is a short, hard-hit, high-bouncing ball that carries out beyond the baseline.

The *backhand overhead smash* is used when the player cannot run around the ball to hit a forehand smash. To begin a backhand overhead, the player should use an eastern backhand or continental grip, and turn the shoulder with the racket side actually facing the net. The elbow on the racket side is up and points to the ball, while the racket head is below the hand. The weight is on the player's back foot and the head is up, eyes fixed on the ball. The ball is contacted above the head slightly in front of the racket shoulder, with the racket face moving through the ball with a strong break of the wrist. The weight is transferred forward through the ball, with the follow through carrying the racket head downward and parallel to the court surface (Figures 5.7–5.9).

The *incorporation of the overhead smash into the total game* blends favorably with the total game plan of a player. The overhead is the second type of shot that is hit before the ball bounces, thus joining the volley shot as

> ### Answer The Telephone
> *Think of the handle of the racket as a telephone and place it by your ear in order to set up immediately for an overhead smash.*

Backhand Overhead Smash

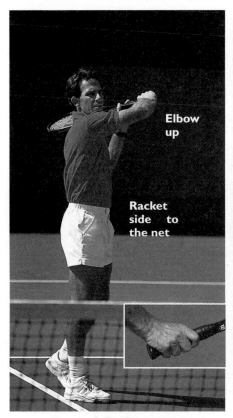

Figure 5.7 Preparation (eastern backhand grip).

Figure 5.8 Contact.

Figure 5.9 Follow through.

Play the Ball
Like an Outfielder

An outfielder in baseball gets under the ball with the glove up in order to catch a fly ball, just as a tennis player should get under the ball with hand up in order to hit an overhead smash.

a stroke hit in the air near the net. When a player is at the net, the opponent must either hit a groundstroke that hopefully can be volleyed by the net player, or a lob that the net player can return as an overhead smash. The player, with improving skill and confidence, can hit an overhead from any location on the court, while the beginning player should hit overheads when lobs are short between the service court line and the net. The beginning player would also be wise to let the ball bounce before executing an overhead so that timing can aid in the stroke. As skill is developed, overheads should be hit on the fly, and the scissors kick should be added. Regardless of skill development, the player needs to remember that the overhead smash is an offensive shot that must be hit under control and with confidence. The player should also remember that the overhead is a first in a series of overheads if the opponent returns the first overhead. Returns of overheads tend to be shorter lobs than the first lob hit, consequently, setting up the player at the net for an eventually "easy" overhead.

LEARNING EXPERIENCE SUGGESTIONS

Orthodox Forehand Overhead Smash

1. The forehand overhead smash is a basic throwing action that imitates the flat serve.

2. The racket head must be placed between the shoulder blades on the backswing.

3. The non-racket arm should point at the ball for a reference point to the ball.

4. The non-racket side of the body is turned, and the back is arched.

5. The base of the orthodox overhead is wide and should remain wide throughout the stroke.

6. The racket is brought through the ball with a wrist snap and a downward follow through.

7. The ball should be "bounced" when it is lobbed extremely high or is hit short to the net.

LEARNING EXPERIENCE SUGGESTIONS

Backhand Overhead Smash

1. The racket elbow should be pointed at the ball on the backhand overhead, and the racket side should be turned to the net during the preparation phase.

2. The wrist should be brought through the ball forcefully on the backhand overhead smash.

THE ELIMINATION OF ERRORS (Forehand Overhead Smash or Backhand Overhead Smash)

The Error	What Causes The Error	Correction of the Error
Hitting into the net.	Ball is too far out in front of the lead shoulder.	Get directly underneath the ball.
Hitting out beyond the baseline of the opponent.	Hitting too hard with poor timing, or hitting up into the ball.	Get directly underneath the ball and hit through the ball with the elbow up.
Inconsistency in placement of the ball.	Racket not placed between the shoulder blades on the backswing, and player's position under the ball is random.	Get directly underneath the ball and always place the racket between the shoulder blades.
Ball is hit off the edge of the racket at the top, or off the bottom edge, causing the ball to be hit long or to hit the court surface immediately.	Swinging too early or too late.	Point the non-racket arm to the ball for a reference point, check the position of the racket on the backswing, and develop a rhythmical timing to the stroke.

THE LOB

The lob is an extension of the groundstrokes, incorporating the same grip and basic swinging action. Mechanics do require the racket face to open and lift the ball up rather than hit through the ball. Lobs, which are characterized by a high *flight pattern*, can be both offensive and defensive. The flight patterns are different for each type of lob, and the differences are based on the purpose of the stroke and the amount of spin applied to the ball. There are two basic lobs used in tennis; and they are discussed on the following pages and diagrammed in Figure 5.10.

The offensive lob is hit over the outstretched reach of the net player, bouncing near the baseline and kicking on deep toward the fence. The defensive lob has a higher flight pattern and is hit off a strong opposing player return, with an underspin rotation.

The *offensive lob* is hit using an eastern forehand or backhand grip. The racket is brought back low with an extensive knee bend. The racket is brought back with the wrist cocked. The racket then moves into the ball with

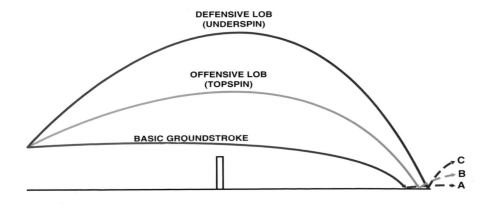

Figure 5.10 Flight patterns of lobs and groundstroke.

a slightly open face at waist height, meeting the ball from underneath and lifting up. The wrist breaks at contact, imparting topspin to the ball. The follow through continues with the racket finishing at an exaggerated high position off the middle of the body, with a roll of the wrist (Figures 5.11–5.16).

Forehand Offensive Lob with Topspin

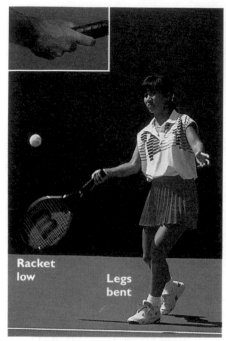

Figure 5.11   Prior to contact (eastern forehand grip).

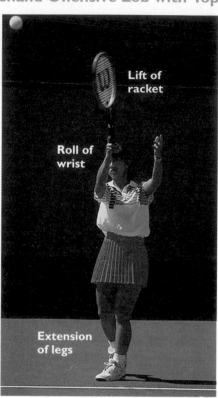

Figure 5.12   Just after contact.

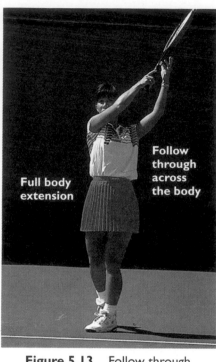

Figure 5.13   Follow through.

Backhand Offensive Lob with Topspin

Figure 5.14   Preparation (eastern backhand grip).

Figure 5.15   Contact.

Figure 5.16   Follow through.

The *defensive lob* is a reaction, in many situations, to an opponent's overhead smash. With an eastern forehand or backhand grip, the racket is brought back into a short backswing position with a firm wrist. The racket is brought forward to hit the ball off the lead shoulder. The bottom edge of the racket leads, opening the racket face. The follow through is high, with the racket face remaining open. The racket stays in the same plane as during the swing from preparation to contact. The wrist remains firm throughout the stroke, and the weight transfer, although important, is minimal compared with other strokes. The legs are bent and extended through the swing pattern, but only with a minimum amount of change. The lob is a reaction to an aggressively hit ball, and the total stroke has to be in moderation to combat the high velocity of the ball (Figures 5.17–5.24).

> ### Hit Over The Pyramid
> *Visualize a pyramid at the apex of the net and hit your defensive lob over that apex. A defensive lob hit with height at the apex of the net will bounce in-court and deep.*
>
> B. Hartwick, Tennis, 11/91, p. 28

Defensive Lob with Forehand Underspin

Figure 5.17 Preparation (eastern forehand grip).

Figure 5.18 Stepping into the ball.

Figure 5.19 Contact.

Figure 5.20 Follow through.

Defensive Lob with Backhand Underspin

Figure 5.21 Preparation (eastern backhand grip).

Figure 5.22 Stepping into the ball.

Figure 5.23 Contact.

Figure 5.24 Follow through.

Racket control, weight transfer, and movement of the feet are essential to hitting lobs. Racket control is used to apply topspin of varying degrees, underspin, or a simple block of the ball.

Weight transfer, as with all shots, is important with the lob, but the transfer has more to do with the hips and a little step transfer rather than with a long step into the ball. It is more of a center of gravity movement forward. Most lobs are hit on the move rather than from a stationary position. The player is either retreating from the net to hit the ball or is moving laterally along the baseline. As a result of having to hit a lob on the run, the lob isn't always a nice setup from a ready position that permits an easy execution of the stroke. Moving the feet to get to the ball, then recovering enough to place the racket on the ball, while attempting to hold form, are all based on the initial foot movement and anticipation as to the location that the opponent has intended for target (Figures 5.24–5.30).

Retreating to Hit a Lob Behind the Baseline — Forehand

Figure 5.25 Backswing.

Figure 5.26 Contact.

Figure 5.27 Follow through.

Retreating to Hit a Lob Behind the Baseline — Backhand

Figure 5.28 Backswing.

Figure 5.29 Contact.

Figure 5.30 Follow through.

The *incorporation of the lob into the total game* is important to the developing player. Without the lob, there is no response to the overhead smash, and the options to hitting a ball when the opponent is at the net are decreased by one. The lob also serves as an occasional change-of-pace stroke, and it can be frustrating for the opponent who likes pace associated with the game or who cannot hit an overhead effectively. The lob is an extension of a groundstroke, and developing the skill is only a transition rather than development of a totally new stroke.

LEARNING EXPERIENCE SUGGESTIONS
Lobs

1. An offensive lob with topspin requires a rolling of the forearm from contact through follow through.

2. All lob follow throughs are to finish high.

3. The more defensive a lob, and the more change from some topspin to an underspin, the more firm the wrist and shorter the backswing.

4. Applying an underspin to a ball on the defensive lob requires a follow through in the same plane.

5. Leg bend and extension are a part of an offensive lob, but the degree relates to the amount of topspin. The more topspin, the more leg bend and extension.

6. The racket face must be open on lobs at contact.

7. It is important to move to the ball as quickly as possible so that form can be incorporated into the stroke.

THE ELIMINATION OF ERRORS (Lobs)

The Error	What Causes The Error	Correction of the Error
Lobs hit long beyond the opponent's baseline.	Too much velocity and lift applied to the ball.	The lob requires touch and feel. Focus on a shorter target.
Balls hit short just over the net.	Usually not enough follow through and backswing.	If stroking the lob, rather than blocking, the backswing and follow through should be equal in distance, and the more distance, the farther the ball will travel.
Lobs that are blocked rebound off at different angles.	Racket face isn't square to the ball.	Provide a firm arm and wrist base with a flat racket face angled for the rebound. Make sure that the forehand grip is a western grip.

Physical Aspects of Playing Tennis

The physical aspects of playing tennis begin to play a major role in performance when you can maintain a rally, keeping the ball in play for a significant amount of time. At that point, you should physically prepare to play the game through a series of stretches and tennis-hitting warm-ups. Overall fitness development and prevention and care of tennis injuries are also important aspects of preparing to play the game.

PHYSICALLY PREPARING TO PLAY TENNIS

There are three phases to physically preparing to play: stretching as a warm-up to hitting the ball, the basic tennis warm-up, and the warm-down through stretching. The first two are designed to actually prepare the player to play, while the third, the warm-down, enables the player to deactivate and decrease muscle stimulation.

When *stretching*, most young players give a cursory effort to preparation of the muscles. However, the young body needs to establish a stretching routine that will be part of the total playing habit into middle age and beyond. It should be incorporated into the player's routine as that player continues to improve and place more stress on the body with extended rallies and overall court play development. The recommended stretching includes some ballistic movement along with static stretching. If the player will devote just five minutes to these warm-up efforts, the risk of injury will be diminished, preparation for the hitting warm-up will be complete, and the body will feel relaxed and prepared to engage in a competitive situation.

Research indicates that prior to stretching the muscles should have engaged in some physical work. The work prescribed is a two minute run or three minutes of running in place. Following the brief running, stretching should begin with concentration on stretching neck flexors and extensors, ligaments of the cervical lumbar spine, ligaments of the shoulder joint, deltoid and pectoral muscles, abdominal muscles, muscles of the hip, muscles and ligaments of the pelvic area, quadriceps and hamstring of the upper leg, gastrocnemius and soleus muscles of the lower leg, and the Achilles' tendon.

There are eleven recommended stretching exercises for tennis presented on the following pages. Each is described by the action required for execution and identified by area to be stretched. The basis for most of these exercises is extrapolated from Werner W. K. Hoeger's *Lifetime Physical Fitness & Wellness - A Personalized Program.* Morton Publ. Co., 1992.

LATERAL HEAD TILT

Action: Tilt the head slowly and gently to one side and hold the stretch for a few seconds. Alternate to the other side and repeat.

Areas Stretched: Flexors and extensors and ligaments of the cervical spine.

SIDE STRETCH

Action: Feet spread at shoulder width with hands on hips. Rotate the body to one side and repeat the process to the other side. Hold the stretch for a few seconds on each side.

Areas Stretched: Pelvis area muscles and ligaments.

ADDUCTOR STRETCH

Action: Feet spread twice shoulder width with hands placed slightly above the knee. Flex one knee and go down to approximately 90 degrees. Hold the stretch and then repeat on the other side.

Area Stretched: Hip adductor muscles.

HEEL CORD STRETCH

Action: Stand against a solid object and stretch the heel downward. Hold the stretch for a few seconds and change legs.

Areas Stretched: Achilles' tendon, gastrocnemius and soleus muscles.

QUAD STRETCH

Action: Stand up straight, grasp the front of the ankle and flex the knee until the heel of the foot is touching the gluteal area. Hold the stretch for a few seconds and change legs.

Areas Stretched: Quadriceps muscle, and knee and ankle ligaments.

SINGLE-KNEE TO CHEST STRETCH

Action: Lie flat on a padded surface. Bend one leg at approximately 100 degrees and place both hands on the lower portion of the knee of the opposite leg, pulling that knee toward the chest. Hold the stretch at the chest level.

Area Stretched: Lower back and hamstring muscles, and the lumbar spine ligaments.

CURLS

Action: Lie flat on padded surface and bend knees at a 90 degree angle. Place arms across chest and curl the upper body to the knees. Repeat the process 15-20 times.

Area Exercised: Abdominal muscles.

SHOULDER HYPEREXTENSION STRETCH

Action: Grasp the throat of the racket with hands close together. Slowly bring the arms up to as close to a perpendicular position to the shoulders as possible. Hold the stretch for a few seconds.

Areas Stretched: Deltoid and pectoral muscles and ligaments of the shoulder joint.

SERVING MOTION ROTATION AND STRETCH

Action: Start with the head of the tennis racket between the shoulder blades and rotate through the service motion. Hold the stretch on the follow through for a few seconds and repeat the process.

Areas Stretched: Upper and lower back area.

SEMI GROUNDSTROKE BODY ROTATION

Action: Place the feet approximately shoulder width apart, grasp the racket with your hands, and with the arms away from the body rotate the trunk as far as possible and hold the stretch. Repeat the rotation the other direction, and continue to follow the same process several times.

Areas Stretched: Hips, abdominal, chest, back, neck, shoulder muscles, and hip spinal ligaments.

SERVING SHOULDER AND ARM STRETCH

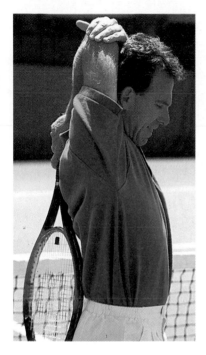

Action: Place the tennis racket head in the small of the back with the elbow in an up position. Place the non-racket hand below the elbow and apply minimal pressure to place the shoulder area on stretch. Hold the stretch for a few seconds and repeat the process several times.

Areas Stretched: Ligaments of the shoulder joint and ligaments of the cervical and lumbar spine.

There are a few final thoughts in regard to stretching prior to playing a tennis match. First, a second reminder that you must have already done some aerobic work to have warmed up before stretching. Second, the range of the stretch is to be done within your comfort zone. Third, the intensity of the stretch should never be painful. And fourth, the duration of a stretch should only be for a few seconds.

The basic tennis warm-up follows the stretching exercises. The warm-up is designed to increase circulation and respiration, and to provide a grooving of tennis strokes. A good warm-up should last 15 minutes, and at the conclusion, both players should be perspiring profusely. A 15-minute warm-up is often shortened due to a player wanting to start the game immediately or having a limited amount of court time available. The beginning player should always work on strokes to be used in the match when warming up. The players should be partners in the warm-up — giving as well as receiving — and attempting to insure that the other partner has had the opportunity for a sound warm-up. The sequence to every tennis warm-up includes:

1. Groundstrokes
2. One player hits groundstrokes, the other volleys, then switch.
3. One player hits lobs while the other hits overheads, then switch.
4. One player hits service while the other player retrieves the serves, then switch (note: there is no return of service — that takes time and detracts from the total warm-up effort).

Although the sequence may differ depending on the location of the players geographically, the concept is reasonably standard.

Finally, at the conclusion of the match and while the players are talking to each other, a *warm-down stretching* activity should be completed. The stretching exercises identified include:

1. Side stretch.
2. Adductor stretch.
3. Heel cord stretch.
4. Quad Stretch.

As part of the warm-down, you should put on a warm-up top and pants and cool down by walking for a period of time prior to sitting down for a rest. As a beginning player this part of warm-down may be a problem, since you have not invested in warm-up clothing, but you should at least put on a jacket following the match. Needless to say, if you happen to have completed a match in 100-degree humid weather, you certainly do not need to put on a jacket.

OVERALL FITNESS DEVELOPMENT

Fitness development of tennis can range from simplistic to sophisticated through the use of programs including weight training, aerobic exercise and interval training. Tennis players who are willing to run, incorporate a sensible exercise program, and work on drills in tennis that incorporate agility and quickness will establish an advantage over individuals who neglect their tennis fitness development.

Cross training by adding running of long distances a minimum of four times per week will enhance the aerobic endurance training necessary for tennis. If the drills used in Chapter 11 of *Tennis Practice By Yourself and with a Partner* are used on a regular basis conditioning, quickness and agility will be improved. In addition, if the player will minimally participate in a strength training workout (without weights) overall fitness will be improved. Exercises to be included in such a workout include push ups, sit ups, modified dips, pull ups, arm curls, and heel raises.

For those who wish to increase their strength training workout a weight training program can be developed that will contribute to potential success of any tennis player by further establishing strength and endurance. There are several choices regarding weight training programs that include free weights, Universal Gym Equipment strength training exercises, and cam (an example is Cybex Strength Training Equipment) strength training exercises. The two that are briefly focused on below are the Universal Strength Training workout which provides a fixed and variable resistance, and the Cybex Strength Training workout which provides a variable resistance workout.

The basic exercises that most contribute to tennis when using the Universal Strength Training Equipment include: arm curls, leg presses, sit ups on an incline board, bench presses, leg curls, lateral pull down, heel raises, and tricep extension. The Cybex strength training equipment enhances tennis strength conditioning through a set of workouts on machines. Each of these workouts is described and presented below with an explanation of the action required for execution and the muscle group developed. When you use these exercises it is important to remember they should be done with a smooth slow action from start to completion.

ABDOMINAL CRUNCH

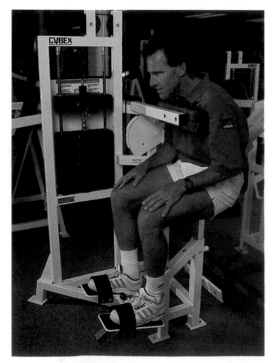

Action: Sit in an upright position with chest against padded bar. Bring chest down toward knees.

Muscle Group: Abdominals

SHOULDER PRESS

Action: Sit upright and grasp handles. Press up until arms are fully extended and return to start.

Muscle Group: Triceps, deltoid, pectoralis major, trapezius, cervatus anterior

CHEST PRESS

Action: Sit upright and press arms forward until extended. Return to start.

Muscle Groups: Pectoralis major, triceps, deltoid

BACK EXTENSION

Action: Slowly press back until the back is fully extended.

Muscle Groups: Erector spinae, gluteus maximus

LAT PULL DOWN

Action: From a sitting position hold the bar with a wide grip and pull bar down until it touches the base of the neck.

Muscle Groups: Latissimus dorsi, pectoralis major, biceps brachioradialis, and trapezius

TRICEP EXTENSION

Action: Sit upright and grasp handles. Press down to full extension and return to start.

Muscle Group: Triceps

ARM CURL

Action: Sit upright and grasp grips with palms up and arms extended. Curl up as far as possible and return to start.

Muscle Groups: Biceps, brachiobrachialis, brachialis, and radialis

LEG PRESS

Action: Lie with flat back on surface, grasp handles and extend legs fully. Return to start.

Muscle Groups: Quadriceps, gluteals

LEG EXTENSION

Action: Lie flat with feet under the bar and extend legs until straight.

Muscle Group: Quadriceps

LEG CURLS

Action: Lie face down with legs under the bar. Curl up at least 90 degrees and return to start.

Muscle Group: Hamstring

HIP/BACK

Action: Stand upright with leg over the bar and press down to full extension. Return to start.

Muscle Group: Gluteus maximus

Regardless of which system you use a workout three days per week with 3–5 sets of ten repetitions will provide a balance of strength and endurance training. One of the exciting aspects of any of the weight programs identified above is that most colleges and universities have facilities established for your choice of weight training work out, and some of those facilities now have state of the art equipment.

As with the various stretching exercises previously mentioned in this chapter the basis for the weight training exercises have been modified for tennis and recommended from Hoeger's *Lifetime Physical Fitness & Wellness* text. You are encouraged to review Hoeger's material for more in-depth information.

SPORTS MEDICINE AND THE PREVENTION AND CARE OF TENNIS INJURIES

There are numerous injuries associated with tennis, and most of them can be prevented. Serious injuries related to contact sports including concussions, cartilage and ligament damage of the knee, shoulder separations, and neck injuries are seldom found in tennis. However, knee, shoulder and back injuries are increasing in number with most of the blame for these injuries placed on hard tennis court surfaces. As a general rule, injuries that do occur in tennis are usually of a mild type that seldom restrict a player's participation. Those few serious injuries that do occur often can be prevented.

Some *minor common tennis injuries are prevented* with a little attention. Blisters often occur on hands and feet and are caused by moisture, pressure, or friction. Feet that slide in a tennis shoe develop blisters. Prevention requires wearing two pair of socks with the cotton pair worn closest to the skin. Blisters on the racket hand are often caused by the racket turning in the hand of the player. You can prevent this type of blister from developing by making sure you have the correct grip size. Usually a larger grip will enable a player to prevent a racket from turning in the hand. Blisters also occur on the racket hand by extensive play when the hand has not been accustomed to that amount of play. The "wear and tear" creates a "hot spot" that results in a blister. Prevention would dictate being conscious of length of playing time and placing some limit to over-extending playing time.

Sometimes a player is bruised when hit by a ball or racket. The only way to avoid this injury is not to assume a position on the court that would provide an opportunity to be hit or to avoid being hit in vulnerable spots of the body. For example, if you are on the direct opposite side of the net from the opposing player and the opposing player is about to hit an overhead smash in line with your position on the court, it is prudent for you to turn and duck. Although a player is hit by a ball on occasion, some bruising also occurs when a player follows through with the racket and hits the shin when serving or when doubles partners swing at the same ball and hit each other. A *hematoma*, a severe bruising, can be caused by these incidents.

In unusually warm and humid weather, when body fluid and salt are lost rapidly, a player may experience cramps. Cramps involve contraction of a muscle or muscle group, causing spasms usually in the abdominal area or gastrocnemius (calf muscle). Prevention of a serious cramping problem is very important. Consume fluids in large quantities. Water is perhaps the best choice of liquids, but diluted fruit juices are an excellent alternative. Sports drinks (Gatorade, Exceed, etc.) also are an alternative; they replace carbohydrates and electrolytes while also replenishing liquid. The key to liquid consumption on a hot and humid day is to drink and then drink more (S. F. Fiske, February, 1992, Tips from the Pros, *Tennis*, p. 83).

More *serious tennis injuries require professional care. Pulled muscles*, including the groin, hamstring, and gastrocnemius generally occur as a result of poor stretching. They can often be avoided by going through a full warm-up.

A *sprained ankle* does occur in tennis and usually happens when the player tries to make a quick turn without the foot following in the turn. Sometimes a player will jump to hit a ball with a scissors kick on the overhead smash and land on the side of the foot or a player will step on a ball during play. Pivoting incorrectly or landing on the side of the foot are a matter of not coordinating effort and physical skill. Stepping on the ball is controllable. Only three tennis balls should be available for play at any one point in a match. If one ball is in play during a rally, there are only two other balls that can become a problem. Court awareness is important. You should keep your side of the court clean by picking up or pushing balls on the court to the net or fence. You also should be aware of a ball that comes from another court and stop play if the ball is in your court area in order to avoid injury. Tennis players are "lazy" when it comes to picking up loose tennis balls, and injury can be the end result.

Knees and wrists also can be injured when playing tennis. Knee ligament and cartilage damage can occur from the same situations that cause an ankle sprain. Stepping on a ball or backpeddling rather than turning a shoulder and running back to a position to return a shot are typical situations that result in these types of injuries.

Shin splints also are an injury that can be associated with tennis because the constant pounding, running, jumping and landing on a hard court creates an inflammation of the soft tissues of the lower legs. A change of tennis court surfaces, high arches, tight calves, and intensity in your workouts and playing situations can all be contributing factors to this injury. Prevention includes being aware of the causes, stretching, and using common sense regarding playing intensity and type of court you are playing on. Selection of the proper shoe with arch support and excellent shock absorption capabilities is also important. Rest and the application of ice when shin splints are in the acute stage are recommended ways of dealing with a shin splint injury (D. Higdon, June, 1992, How to prevent shin splints, *Tennis*, p. 102).

Repetitive twisting and trunk rotation is a part of tennis. When the trunk accelerates through on groundstrokes or the overhead arching motion required in a serve or overhead is executed, the risk for *back injury* increases. In addition, hard court surfaces can be damaging as well. Preventive measures for back injury include conditioning programs and good stroke technique. Professional help following a back injury includes rehabilitation through an athletic trainer or a physical therapist who specializes in sport medicine (D. Squires, April, 1993, Oh, my aching back, *Tennis USTA*, p. 10).

Two injuries that seem to be quite common in tennis have different causes. The *Achilles' tendon* is sometimes injured by simple physical actions, such as jumping and landing on the ball of the foot without lowering the heel or by pushing off the ball of the foot, thus placing extreme pressure on the tendon. The tendon, if ruptured, sounds like a gunshot retort, and the player becomes immediately immobile. Ridged, high-arched feet with heels that angle inward or flat feet that roll inward are often most vulnerable to Achilles' tendon problems. The Achilles' tendon often is chronically sore, because players ignore persistent, tolerable pain and continue to play. The Achilles' tendon, and the sheath that surrounds it, becomes inflamed and soreness, swelling and pain are the outcome. Ignoring these signs can cause severe problems, and the only way to address the injury is to stop playing and rest. Prevention, on the other hand, can be important and includes stretching the Achilles' tendon in warm-up and warm-down. Orthotics for your shoe, or heel pads, also are used as a preventive measure, but elevating your heel also shortens the tendon when what is needed is to lengthen the tendon. As a result, stretching becomes even more important if a heel pad is used. Once an Achilles' tendon injury has occurred, rehabilitation includes rest and modality application. Modalities used in therapy include ice, massage, ultrasound or electrical stimulation, and are used to reduce swelling and begin rehabilitation that brings the Achilles' tendon back to a normal condition. A stiff or achy tendon is a sign of an impending rupture, and if you rupture an Achilles' tendon, there is a very long process of rehabilitation following surgery or immobilization (A. McNab, June, 1993, Protecting your Achilles', *Tennis*, p. 99).

The other common tennis injury is *tennis elbow*, an injury that carries status and pain. There are several types of tennis elbow injuries, the main characteristic being an inflammation of the elbow area. The injury can be prevented if a player uses proper skill techniques and strokes. Hitting with the elbow leading on the backhand or hitting numerous slice or spin serves will provide ample opportunity for the injury to occur. Prevention requires correction of poor mechanics along with common sense regarding how many spin serves you are going to hit. Treatment of an elbow injury is restricted to rest or the application of a support. Elbow supports and splints are available to relieve minor pain from tennis elbow, but they will not eliminate the cause.

If an injury is perceived as serious, a physician should be consulted as soon as possible. If rehabilitation is recommended, it is advisable to seek out a sports medicine clinic. Most metropolitan areas have centers that work closely with physicians to rehabilitate injuries.

Home treatment should be limited to only minor injuries. Blisters usually dry up on their own; the main concern is to make sure that they do not get infected. For minor injuries, some athletic trainers can develop devices to enable continuation of activity. For example, a donut-shaped pad can be devised by a trainer that will cover a blister that will reduce the pain at the pressure point and avoid additional friction on the blister area. Bruises often can be treated with cold compresses or ice packs to reduce swelling. For injuries such as Achilles' tendon, tennis elbow, and pulled muscles, rest may be the only solution.

Mental Aspects of Tennis Competition

7

It obviously takes physical effort and mental planning of strategy to be successful in tennis. Without the physical skill, an individual would have a very difficult time winning. The mental state, however, goes beyond physical skill — it actually replenishes the physical effort. The mental effort that controls the tennis match is the intangible that accents the physical and gives direction to the purpose of playing tennis. The mental aspects of tennis are the true key to success on a tennis court.

A beginning tennis player should ask "Why participate in a game that requires so much from a player, both physically and mentally?" To play tennis requires a bit of a childlike personality. The player has to want to play for play's sake. Associated with that concept is the acceptance of playing for fun and for the sheer joy of physical movement and abandonment. The tennis player needs to feel the game, feel the esthetics, and appreciate the execution of skill. Playing for fitness or even skill development, and playing for fun, contribute to the special feeling of participating in tennis for the right reasons. A player should feel the sun and breeze caressing the body and absorb the sound of balls striking rackets, the chatter of people, and the sounds of effort as a player reaches for an overhead or completes a serve. Tennis is not bigger than life. It isn't life itself, and it is never a life or death situation. Tennis is a life experience that can enhance your self-worth and self- esteem; it is about your inner self (J. Loehr, April, 1989, Picture this, *World Tennis*, p. 22). If the game is played for the correct reasons, all the other parts, including winning, fall into place.

UNDERSTANDING WHAT COMPETITION REALLY MEANS

Competition and winning are often confused as being the same, but they are barely related. In competition, winning is a by-product for at least one of the participants. Competition is not opponent against opponent — it is player against barrier. If the tennis player can visualize that the player on the other side of the net is providing barriers, an understanding of competition begins to emerge. The opponent — through a serve, a volley, or a lob — is placing a barrier for the other player to respond to in an effective manner. The barrier is placed in front of a player for a challenge. It is nothing personal, and a tennis player must see that to be really successful in a match, and to learn to truly compete.

A player must learn to emphasize *execution over winning*. If execution is the important aspect, the winning will take care of itself. Worrying about winning or losing interferes with both execution and winning. Thinking about appearances or pleasing others interferes with execution and winning. The emphasis is on execution, the concentration is on execution, and the goal is execution. A clarification is in order when the term "execution" is used. The emphasis is not on thinking about executing a skill pattern — it is on completing the skill pattern. The mind should be focused on feeling a barrier and responding to it by a reflex action, and that reflex action is execution. If a player begins to analyze movement and strokes, or begins to think of ulterior motives behind execution, there is a collapse of skilled play. The beginning tennis player may never have been exposed to this concept before and so may have difficulty understanding why thinking about winning is not acceptable. If the player will realize that emphasis on winning places pressure to excel and pressure to not fail, then the idea of eliminating those pressures might become palatable. If executing by doing provides the realization of the long-term goal of winning, then execution begins to make sense.

ELIMINATING NEGATIVE ATTITUDES

A *negative attitude or negative feelings* contribute to a negative response when participating in tennis. If a player is ready to receive a serve and the thought "please don't make the serve; double fault — please" flashes, a very negative attitude has been established. Other thoughts that seem to be a part of the game include "what if I miss the shot," or "if I hold my serve I can win," or "you dummy — why can't you hit the ball?" Each thought plants a seed of negative response that contributes to a less than successful experience. Negative attitudes arise when a player gets upset and begins to talk to the other self: "How could you hit such a stupid shot" or "I can't believe you are real — how could you miss such an easy setup?" If a player keeps making derogatory statements about performance, that player will exceed all expectations of failure through negative thought. *Fear of winning and fear of losing* are both contributing factors to negative thought. Fear places pressure on the player to not make mistakes, and that negative thought reemphasizes fear of failure. The player becomes anxious to do well, and that anxiousness contributes to tension, which restricts performance (since performance must be accomplished in a relaxed, controlled manner).

Becoming *angry and losing one's temper* is another negative. The anger is a means of releasing energy, and this will take a toll on the player when a demand for extra effort is needed and the body cannot provide it. Losing temper also places pressure on that player. A player who gets mad at himself or herself is venting anger internally. That internal anger creates the same anxiety as when there is a fear of winning or losing, with the player trying to please "self." The effect of the cycle of anger-anxiety-pressure is the collapse of the player's performance during competition.

Another negative associated with performance and tennis play is the behavior of the opponent. There is a very popular term in sport — *psyching out*. Behavior by an opponent can be upsetting if permitted to be upsetting. Body language, verbal comments, gamesmanship, and outbursts by an opponent can create negative reaction that will create anxiety for the other player. The feeling of "why did she say that" or "I wish he would shut his mouth" establish negative thought patterns in the other player.

Negative thoughts can be changed by realizing what is happening and replacing them with positive thoughts. Instead of worrying about a missed shot, concentration should focus on remembering a similar shot that was executed well. Instead of hoping that an opponent will miss a serve, a player should demand that the serve be good so that "I can have the opportunity to return a winner." The fear of winning and/or losing is eliminated if the player will remember and practice what competition means and will shut out the emphasis on winning and losing. Certainly attacking one's own person verbally and sometimes physically is not being a friend to the inner self. The developing player should treat the inner self with respect and dignity, stop arguing with and embarrassing one's other self, and begin to compliment the other self on a good shot or a good point played. Finally, not allowing an opponent to apply psyching techniques is extremely helpful in facing competition.

CONCENTRATION

Concentration is a very important part of tennis. Blocking out all factors other than executing a shot is required to have good concentration and ultimate success. Concentration is centered around *focus*. The focus on the ball and the task of hitting the ball, along with the focus on the environment, helps a player to concentrate. When engaged in a rally, the player should look at the seams of the ball all the way to the racket face. Research indicates that a player can only see a ball to within four feet of the racket, but just the effort to look the ball into the racket improves concentration. Concentration is also enhanced by certain environmental situations. One of those is being in touch with one's own body. The ability to synchronize breathing with each stroke, and sensing the heartbeat as a body function, permit the player to be in touch.

Other senses also enhance concentration, including hearing the tennis ball make contact with the racket strings, feeling the impact of ball and racket, and recognizing muscle contraction and tension during the stroke. To really concentrate requires an elimination of all extraneous aspects of the environment. Exchanging sides of the court is a time for concentration and relaxing. The concentration should be on the extension of the game plan and thinking positive thoughts. If a player keeps saying "I am playing well," after awhile that thought becomes reality. Concentration is focusing on the task at hand.

ANXIETY AND SLUMPS

There will be times when everything "clicks" during a game, and there will be a *flow* to movement and to the play in general. That flow may last for a few points in a match, for a larger portion of a match, for a few days, or for months. Then there will be down times, situations where nothing seems to work and where Murphy's Law is for real. The down time is described best as a *slump*, and a slump is caused by *anxiety*. Slumps seem to appear for no reason, but they usually are a result of worrying, tension, or a fear of winning/losing. In short, slumps occur as a result of pressure that is self-induced, and that pressure causes anxiety. Once a player becomes anxious, muscles tense, which in turn, forces physical errors, because there is no relaxation during stroke execution. When the errors mount, tension increases and the slump continues. As long as the player permits the pressure to interfere with performance the cycle will continue.

The cure to the slump is to eliminate the anxiety by reducing muscle tension. This can be done in two ways: 1) the player begins to cope with success and failure and begins to think positive, and 2) the player begins to relax and hit out on each ball, eliminating concern for end result. In order to reduce muscle tension, the player needs to rebuild confidence. Participating in a match with a player who hits with consistent pace is a start at redeveloping that confidence, and self-talks, including "good shot — way to play," aid in raising the self-esteem necessary for self-confidence. Believing that the flow will return and relaxing are keys to coping in a positive manner. As a means of relaxing, the player must work at minimizing the number of times the muscle groups will be permitted to tense, thus decreasing interference with relaxed performance. During competition when the flow is present, it often disappears when the player realizes that "I shouldn't be playing this well." There is a self-fulfilling prophecy that begins to make the player anxious, and the whole cycle within the match begins to develop. An interesting aspect of the prophecy is that in the next match a slump may not be evident, but somewhere in the match, if similar circumstances occur, play will deteriorate just as before. Regardless of the length of the slump, the anxiety causes muscle tension, which reduces performance.

THE CONTRIBUTION OF RELAXATION

The ability to relax contributes greatly to physical performance. Learning how to relax in a tennis match is related to recognizing muscle tension. If the player grips the racket with excessive force (an exception when hitting volley shots), muscle tension is too great. Shoulder and arm muscles that are tight can be recognized with a little practice. Tenseness in the mouth and jaw areas is a common occurrence, and a check of the jaw will reveal this. The whole body can tense during the pressure of a particular point or game, and shortness of breath, excessive sweating, and mental confusion are signals that the stress is too great. Relaxation during play can be attained in several ways: 1) by immediately responding to tension on the court, 2) by preparing to play through mental rehearsal and mental imagery, and 3) by relaxing before the match.

The *immediate response to tension on the court* is to learn how to recognize the tension and then relax those muscle groups. If the player feels tension in the shoulders and neck, a clockwise rotation of the head followed by a counterclockwise motion will relax that area. Tension in the arms and legs can be eliminated by running or skipping in place. Another exercise that aids in total body relaxation is to take a deep breath and hold for a count of five, finally expelling the air.

Preparing to play through the use of *mental rehearsal* or *mental imagery* requires practice, but it can be learned in a short time. The idea is to prepare so well mentally that confidence is enhanced, which, in turn, reduces anxiety and tension. There are several approaches to this way of developing relaxation. One is to correct a skill problem by visualizing the mistake, then repeatedly reviewing the proper skill with the mind. Sometimes the skill problem is more related to the sequence of shots or a game plan, and the corresponding mental practice should be to use imagery emphasizing the acceptable shot or sequence of shots in a game plan. This mental imagery is a foundation for the actual tennis match and will assist the player in recognizing certain situations. Mental rehearsal even helps during a match when a player visualizes a positive picture of the next sequence of serves or a strategy for moving the ball from one side of the court to the other in a baseline rally.

The third form of relaxation is *pre-match relaxation*. The most widely used technique is *progressive relaxation*, which involves developing a habitual twenty-minute-per-day relaxation exercise plus a before-a-match session. Skill development is centered on recognizing muscle tension followed by relaxing each muscle group. The tension recognition and relaxation response provides a foundation to approach both life and tennis on a more relaxed level. This skill carries over to a tennis match by permitting the player to recognize pressure during play, and immediately relaxing enough to prevent a deterioration of performance. Other forms of pre-match relaxation include meditation and self-hypnosis, and are all compatible for use by a tennis player to improve performance. The progressive relaxation technique and additional forms of pre-match relaxation also contribute to the player using mental rehearsal or imagery after attaining a position of relaxation. The mental aspects of tennis preparation can raise the level of a player's skill to an optimum not considered possible. The game is more mental than physical. The developing player must make the effort to understand what competition really is and apply that knowledge in play. If negative thoughts can be eliminated and anxiety reduced, play will improve. If concentration is developed, and various forms of relaxation are applied, the player will improve rapidly. Mental aspects of tennis require that the player change former attitudes of competition and apply the mental to the physical effort in a positive manner. The mental aspect of tennis is a psychological and philosophical approach to playing the game, and to enjoying life through tennis.

MENTAL TOUGHNESS

Jim Loehr (1992) provides an excellent view on mental toughness and insight into the positive approach to mentally preparing for a match. He uses terminology analogous to muscular strength — resilience, strength, flexibility, and responsiveness — to define mental toughness.

Resilience is related to emotional excess baggage you carry into the next point of a match following a mistake. If your skill errors come in bunches, you may struggle with your temper and develop a negative attitude (everything is downhill from here). If a bad call upsets you then you are not a resilient tennis player. To overcome low resilience, focus on the positive. Avoid drooping or whining after a missed shot and turn away from the net, leaving the mistake behind you.

Players with *emotional strength* generate positive emotional support for themselves and reject negative emotional distress. Characteristics of a non-strength oriented player is one who is shy about pumping a fist in the air or showing positive emotion, is fearful of looking an opponent in the eyes, makes a line call softly, or rarely questions an obviously bad call. Emotional strength must be displayed on the court through body language, voice patterns, and general attitude. Opponents sense weak behavior and uncertainty. If you think negatively, your hormones and nervous system respond by generating nervousness and tight muscles. Positive thoughts enable you to use your energy in a productive manner and permits you to be relaxed when executing your shots. The key is to assume a court presence: stand up straight, move with a purpose, use a firm voice in your calls, and stop complaining.

The *flexible* player is a player who creates a relaxed atmosphere in stressful situations. Laughing at a stupid mistake, ignoring poor court conditions or an obnoxious opponent, eliminating tantrums, and looking and feeling positive under all circumstances are signs of a flexible player. Positive thought and action are critical to a player who intends to be flexible.

Finally, a *responsive* player is one who maintains alertness and intensity. Behaviors such as playing in a daze, being too casual, forgetting the score, and not caring, contribute to an unresponsive attitude. A responsive player focuses on the event and maintains a standard of expectation for a high performance level (J. Loehr, July/August, 1992, How to get mentally tough/Part I and II, *Tennis*, pp. 45 and 61).

There is a great deal of mental effort involved when playing tennis. Understanding what competition really is, eliminating negative attitudes, and developing relaxation techniques are extremely helpful to your playing success. In addition, a positive attitude to counteract negative feelings, along with positive mental imagery, contribute as well.

Etiquette and Rules Interpretation

8

Part of playing tennis is understanding the written and unwritten rules of the game. Tennis has been played for centuries, and there are certain ways of behaving and interpreting rules.

BEHAVIOR ON A TENNIS COURT

The unwritten rules of tennis are associated with behavior on a tennis court, or, stated in a more proper form, tennis etiquette. The unwritten rules have evolved over the years, and most of them have a purpose as they relate to tennis.

Appropriate clothing for tennis does not require a major expenditure, but proper dress is part of the game. A tennis player must wear tennis shoes rather than a track type shoe or basketball shoe. Wearing proper shoes reduces the chance of injury, and it prevents marring of the tennis court surface (see Chapter 12 for additional comments related to shoes as equipment). Municipal, private and college courts have rules requiring proper footwear, and players are expected to wear shorts and a shirt to play on those courts. Playing at a private tennis club increases clothing expectations to more conventional styles, including tennis shorts or skirt and a tennis shirt or blouse.

Even the act of picking up a tennis ball has a certain degree of status. Bending over and picking up the ball is, of course, one way to retrieve the ball. Other methods include a foot/racket pickup and a ball-bounce pickup. The *foot/racket pickup* (Figure 8.1) requires that the ball is positioned

Figure 8.1 Foot/racket pickup.

Figure 8.2 Ball bounce pickup.

between the racket side foot and the face of the tennis racket. Simultaneously lift the foot, ball, and racket to mid-calf level, and, as the ball becomes airborne, use the racket to bounce the ball to the court surface and catch with your non-racket hand. The *ball bounce pickup* (Figure 8.2) requires you to choke up on the racket handle and place the racket face on top of the ball. Then lift the racket slightly and contact the ball with a series of quick wrist movements that lift the ball off the court and into your non-racket hand.

Most tennis facilities consist of three or more courts enclosed by a fence, with one or two gates to admit a player. When *walking on a tennis court*, you should wait until play has stopped before proceeding to an assigned court, and you should walk along the fence as quickly as possible. *Talking on a tennis court* is unacceptable except for normal voice tones, and conversation should be limited as much as possible to the match rather than to everyday visiting.

Warm-up is described in Chapter 6 as a part of physically preparing to play. *Being a partner in warm-up* was described as both players receiving an equal opportunity to prepare physically to play. Etiquette insists that each player be willing to help the other warm-up in a fair-minded manner.

How to return tennis balls to another court, and *how to request a return of tennis balls* are also parts of court etiquette. When a tennis ball rolls across a court from an adjacent court while play is in progress, action should stop, and the ball should be returned. The action should be stopped assuming that the rolling ball interferes with the play, and if it does, then the point should be replayed. The ball should be returned to the adjacent court on a bounce to the requesting player. If a ball is hit onto another court, the requesting player should wait until play ceases on that court, and then with a raised hand request "ball please," followed by "thank you" upon receipt of the ball. Balls hit over the fence must be retrieved, but the retrieval must follow the same court behavior as when entering the court for the first time.

Once the *ball is in play* during a match, there should be no interruptions for hitting practice serves. That practice is part of the warm-up and interferes with the flow of the game if done during the first or second games of the match. The server must always begin with two tennis balls. For convenience, one ball should be placed in the pocket of the tennis shorts and one in the hand for the toss. When receiving, the player should hit only a ball that is legally in play. It is poor form to return an "out" serve. When a ball or other interference occurs during a match, a gesture of "play a let" is acceptable. A situation that might make the point is if a server hits the first serve as fault, then a ball rolls across the court. If the receiver responds by picking up the ball and returning it to the adjacent court, the receiver should immediately respond to the server, "take two." Another form of court behavior is to communicate all calls to the opponents in an informative manner. Verbal forms of communication are "out" and "let." A ball that is "in" is assumed "in" by the continued play on the part of the player returning the shot. An index finger pointing up can be used as a sign language for a ball that is out, and a ball hit out of reach of a player that is good is signified by a flat, palm-down motion.

Emotion is to be left off the court! Throwing a racket, hitting an erratic shot after play has stopped, and verbal outbursts should not and do not have to be tolerated. There is an easy way to cope with opponents who behave in such an unacceptable manner, and that is to refuse to play them. Life is too short to accept behavior of a negative type in an environment that is supposed to be designed for fun and fitness. Other unacceptable responses include making excuses for losing while not acknowledging the good play of an opponent, and not keeping score accurately.

Perhaps the most misunderstood part of etiquette is related to a rules interpretation of *when a ball is called "in" or "out" on a line call.* The rule and the etiquette application are simple. A ball that touches any part of a court boundary line is "in" (Figure 8.3) and any time a ball is wholly out by not touching any part of a boundary line, the call is "out" (Figure 8.4). The problem is when players don't see the ball and start making guesses. There is no excuse for guessing — that call is specific! If a player does not see a ball as "out," the ball must be considered playable, and it is communicated as good by continued play. There never is a guess on a line call in tennis — the ball is always good unless seen out. There is one option available to an "unsighted" player. If a player does not see the ball, that player can request that the other player make the call. If the opposing player was "unsighted," or doesn't wish to make the call, the call reverses back to the original player, who must them accept the ball as being in bounds.

Figure 8.3 Ball on the line – "IN."

Figure 8.4 Ball near the line – "OUT."

Besides playing a tennis match and acknowledging etiquette, *viewing a tennis match* requires certain behavior, since a spectator has the obligation to observe a match with respect for the players. There should be no communication between player and spectator, including the often asked question of "What's the score?" The spectator should be quiet and watch the play, and applaud a good point played. Spectator disruptions are not approved for major tennis tournament matches (such as the U.S. Open, professional tour matches, and collegiate competition).

INTERPRETATION OF THE RULES OF TENNIS

An interpretation of the most applicable rules are presented on the following pages.

Tennis court dimensions are not important to know except in general terms, but the *terminology* of the court area is important. Key terms include baseline, center mark, back court, forecourt, right service court, left service court, service line, and the alley. (See Figure 8.5.) Important court dimensions are the singles court size of

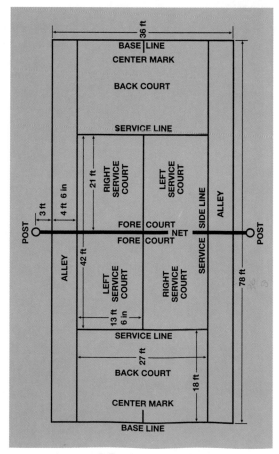

Figure 8.5 Court dimensions.

Figure 8.6   Measurement of the net.

27' × 78' and the expanded doubles court size of 36' × 78'. The net is 3'6" high at the net supports and 3' high at the center. The net height at the center is of particular importance, since a lower or higher height would impact the rally between two players. The measurement of the center net height is done by placing one racket vertically at the center strap position and the other racket horizontally on top of the butt of the first racket's handle. Because most rackets today are oversized, the second string of the horizontal racket should be even with the top of the net for the net to be at the correct height (Figure 8.6).

The *choice of serve, side of court, and order of service* are significant choices to make at the beginning of a match. A decision on *choice of service and side of court* to begin play is made by a spin of the racket or a flip of a coin. A racket spin is done by placing the top of the racket head on the court. The opposing player calls either "up" or "down" to signify the position of the butt end of the racket when it falls to the court. The winner of the spin chooses, or requests the opponent to choose, the right to be the server or receiver. The player who doesn't have first choice then selects the end of the court to begin play. The choices may also be reversed, with the winner of the spin choosing, or requesting the opponent to choose, the end to begin play followed by the non-selecting player's choice of service or receiving serve. A scenario might clarify the choices available: Player A wins the spin and states, "I will serve." Player B then states, "I will take the north side." A second scenario would consist of Player A winning the spin and stating "your choice." Player B then states, "I will receive," followed by Player A's retort of, "I will take the north side." The point is that the first player has the option of choosing service, receipt of serve, or end of the court, or of passing those choices on to the opponent.

The *order of serve* is a simple alternation of serves in either singles or doubles play. A player must serve through a full game, then exchange service with the opponent at the conclusion of that game. In doubles, the same situation exists except that teams alternate serving following each game. If Team I serves the first game, Team II will serve game two, and the rotation process will continue. Player A of Team I serves the first game, Player A of Team II serves the second game, Player B of Team I serves the third game, and Player B of Team II serves the fourth game. The process repeats itself throughout the set with Player A of Team I serving in game number five.

Changing sides of the court needs to be understood, since it has a significant effect on performance when playing outdoors. Without changing the side of court, one player would always face the sun or wind during play. The opponent would thereby have an advantage. Rotation to different sides of the court occurs when the total number of games played is an odd number. If Player A (or Team I) serves from the north side of a court in game number one, sides will be exchanged for game number two. Player B (or Team II) would then serve from the north side of the court, followed by Player A (or Team I) serving game three from the south end of the court. At the conclusion of game number three, the players (or teams) again change sides of the court, with Player B (or Team II) serving from the south side of the court in game number four. The sequence continues with players (or teams) exchanging sides of the court in the fifth, seventh, ninth, and eleventh total games played. At the conclusion of a set, the players or teams only change sides if the total games are an odd number (i.e., 6-3 for a total of nine games). In singles, the rotation of server is continuous throughout the match regardless of sets played. In doubles, the same principle applies with the rotation of each team in order or service, but within a team there can be an exchange of order of serve at the beginning of each new set.

In doubles play, there are rules to control the *location of players while serving and receiving*. Once the serving rotation is determined for a team, as described above, the rotation is permanent until a new set begins. The same is true for a team receiving the serve. One player must always receive from the right service court, and one player must always receive from the left service court. Again, as with serving, change in receiving order may only occur at the start of a new set.

Scoring a game, set, and match accurately is a major responsibility of both players. Scoring when viewed in a systematic order is simple to understand. A tennis match is played in a sequence of points, games, sets, and match. It takes four points to win a game, providing that the margin for victory is by two points. Six games must be won by a player to win a set, with a winning margin of two games. One exception to the rule is that if six games are won by each player, a tie breaker is played to determine the winner, and the final score will always be 7-6 — which is a margin of only one game for the victory. In most situations, the winner of the match is the winner of two of three sets (professional players on the men's tour play three out of five sets in some tournaments).

TABLE 8.1 ● Point Scoring	
Point Number	**Equivalent Term**
First Point	15
Second Point	30
Third Point	40
Fourth Point	Game (must win by two points)
No Points	Love
Tie Score	Deuce
After a tie at 4 points each — server leads	Advantage In (AD IN)
After a tie at 4 points each — receiver leads	Advantage Out (AD OUT)

Each point won by a player is assigned a term as described in Table 8.1. Scores to complete a set are inclusively 6-0, 6-1, 6-2, 6-3, 6-4, 7-5, or 7-6. If a set score reaches 5-5 in terms of games won, two more games must be played. If one player wins both games, the final set is 7-5; if the players split games, the score will be 6-6, and a tie breaker will be played. Examples of a match score are 6-2, 7-5, or 6-3, 1-6, 6-4. The winning player's scores are always identified first in a match; consequently, the 1-6 score of the second set of the second match example indicates that the winner of the match lost the second set by a six-to-one game score.

A *tie breaker* is played only when a set is tied 6-6. There are several forms of tie breakers, including what are called 7, 9, and 12 point tie breakers. The 12 point tie breaker is the most popular, and is presented as follows. The winner of a tie breaker is the first player to win 7 points with a winning margin of 2 points. If the score in a tie breaker reaches 6-6 in number of points scored, then the players must continue the game until one player has a winning margin of two points (i.e., 8-6, 9-7, 10-8, etc.). A 5-5 point score can still produce a winner at seven points if one player wins the next two points.

The server for the first point of a tie breaker is designated by the continued rotation of serve per the normal rotation. The first server serves only one point — from the right service court. The second server begins the serve from the left service court. One point is served from the left service court, then one point from the right service court by the same server. In singles, the service order now reverses back to the first server, who begins service for one point from the left service court, then moves to the right service court for the second point. The players exchange ends of court after a total of six points is played, with a continuation of the rotation.

In doubles play rotation, movement is the same as in singles except that four players are involved instead of two. Player A of Team I serves point number one to the right service court. Player A of Team II serves two points — one from the left service court followed by one from the right service court. Player B of Team I then serves points one and two from the respective left and right service courts, and the rotation continues to Player B of Team II, etc. The tie breaker singles and doubles rotation is found in Table 8.2.

Placing the ball in play is sometimes misunderstood by players, so a clarification is in order. The start of every game is initiated with a service to the right service court. The service point, both in a regular game situation or

TABLE 8.2 ● Tie Breaker Server Rotation

SINGLES				DOUBLES			
Player Number	Service Court to Serve To	Number of Points	Team No.	Player No.	Service Court to Serve To	Number of Points
1	Right Service Court	1	1	A	Right Service Court	1
2	Left Service Court	1	2	A	Left Service Court	1
2	Right Service Court	1	2	A	Right Service Court	1
1	Left Service Court	1	1	B	Left Service Court	1
1	Right Service Court	1	1	B	Right Service Court	1
2	Left Service Court	1	2	B	Left Service Court	1
------ change sides of court ------			------ change sides of court ------			
2	Right Service Court	1	2	B	Right Service Court	1
1	Left Service Court	1	1	A	Left Service Court	1
1	Right Service Court	1	1	A	Right Service Court	1
etc.			etc.			

a tie breaker, includes a maximum of two opportunities to hit a legal serve. There is one exception, and that is when a *let* is played. A let is a serve that is hit in all ways legally except that the ball touches the net on its path to the service court. A let permits the server to repeat that one particular serve, and any number of lets may be played in succession.

Once the *ball is in play*, it must be hit by a player on one side of the court and cross the net on the fly landing in the opponent's court. During a rally, players may hit the ball on the bounce or during flight (return of serve follows the bounce of the ball in the service court). Balls that bounce twice before being returned, a ball hit out of the court boundaries on the fly, balls that hit the net and do not go over the net, and two serves in a row that do not fall into the appropriate service court are all related to a loss of a point.

A serve that does not strike the appropriate service court is described as a *fault*. Servers also fault by swinging and missing a service toss, and by stepping on the baseline during the serve. Touching the service line on a serve is called a *foot fault*. Many players have the habit of touching the baseline in this manner, and legally that is not accepted. If a player strikes the ball, then comes down on the baseline, the serve is legal. When the foot touches the line while the racket is in contact with the ball, or prior to hitting the ball, the serve is lost. In "friendly" play, foot faults are usually not called since they are difficult to see. But the server has a responsibility to avoid the illegal foot position.

There are numerous rule infractions and interpretations in tennis. Some of them are listed below:

1. Hitting a volley prior to the ball crossing the net is a loss of point except when a ball crosses the net and the wind blows, or backspin carries the ball back across the net.

2. A ball that strikes the player or the player's clothing is considered a loss of a point.

3. The player may not throw a racket at the ball. The penalty is loss of the point.

4. If the ball strikes the net, excluding the serve, and continues on into the opponent's court, the ball is still in play.

5. If a doubles player hits the partner with the ball, the team loses the point.

6. A receiver of a serve must be ready for service, or the serve must be repeated.

7. An opposing player may not hinder an opponent by distracting the opponent, however, partners on a doubles team are allowed to talk to each other when the ball is directed to their side of the court.

8. A player hit by a ball prior to the ball striking the court loses that point even if the ball is going to land out of bounds.

9. After the conclusion of a tie breaker, the first server of the next set is the player who did not serve first in the previously played set.

A complete review of tennis rules is found in the Appendix. A copy can be obtained by writing to the United States Tennis Association, Publications Department, 70 West Red Oaks Lane, White Plains, New York 90604.

The beginning tennis player should remember to treat the rules with dignity and take them seriously so that the game will be enjoyable.

Singles Strategy

Strategy in singles is part physical and part mental. The physical provides the mechanics to execute what the mental suggests be done to win a point. The mental is divided into two parts: 1) thinking and broadening thought to plan for the whole match, and 2) using the mind to control the match. This chapter is concerned with the physical or mechanical execution of what the mental suggests and requires in developing a game plan. The mental part related to controlling the match is discussed in Chapter 7.

PERCENTAGE TENNIS

Tennis is a game of mistakes, and the player that makes the most mistakes loses. To win at tennis, it takes a concept described as *percentage tennis*. Percentage tennis is specific to hitting every ball deep and within the lines of the tennis court. This sounds easy, and, in fact, it is if the player is devoted to the system of play. The problem with percentage tennis is that players would rather hit the one spectacular shot than play the ball methodically. A percentage player is one who plays within the limits of skill, hitting only the shots that skill development will permit. In addition, the percentage player hits the appropriate stroke for a given shot. There are two considerations that a percentage tennis player should grasp. The first is to comprehend what shot should be hit from what position on the court, and the second is to understand and be able to apply the division theory of play.

Court Division For Position Play Strategy

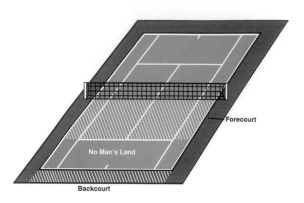

Figure 9.1   Court division for position play.

The tennis court is divided into three parts: backcourt, wasteland, and forecourt (Figure 9.1). The backcourt extends a yard deep behind the baseline, and this is where the percentage player returns all deeply hit shots from the opponent. The percentage concept requires that the player be a wall board returning every shot from the backcourt deep to the opponent's court. The forecourt is between the service court line and the net, and all shots in this area are either volleys, overhead smashes, or approach shots. This is the area that the player should enjoy, because a ball hit in the forecourt represents an opponent's error, which permits the percentage player to control the net area. The wasteland is the portion of the court where the percentage player must step to return a shot, then retreat to the baseline to play the next shot. A player should never stand in the wasteland. It is a highly vulnerable area and should be avoided.

Understanding and Application of the Division Theory of Play Strategy

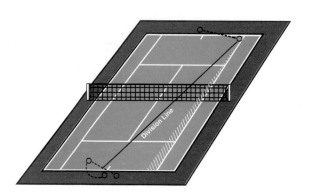

Figure 9.2   Division theory of play.

A second consideration in percentage tennis is to understand and apply the *division theory of play* (Figure 9.2). This involves dividing the court into two parts on every stroke. If two players are rallying from the baseline and the ball is coming straight back to each player, the court is divided at the center mark on the baseline. If the opposing player hits a ball angled to the left of the percentage player, and the ball lands near the sideline halfway between the service court line and the baseline, and then the return is a comparable cross-court return, the division line for the percentage player, upon return to the baseline, is a step and a half to the left of the center mark of that baseline. The theory is to force the opposing player to hit a low percentage shot for a winner, or to return the ball to the percentage player who is situated such that the rest of the court is covered equally with a forehand or backhand shot.

If the percentage player can stay out of the wasteland except to return a shot, can apply the division line theory, and can hit each return deeply at least three times in a row, the percentage of the opposing player losing the point is quite high. When hitting from the baseline, the percentage player should use the topspin groundstroke when possible due to the high safe trajectory and the deep, abrupt drop of the ball at the far baseline.

SERVICE AND SERVICE RETURN STRATEGY

The use of the *service as a part of strategy* is a necessity. Most beginners breathe a sigh of relief when their serve strikes the appropriate service court. Strategy occurs when the serve strikes the service court because the server had confidence, hit the ball with velocity, and had a plan as to where the ball would be placed in the service court. If a server can repeatedly hit a serve with a modest amount of speed and place the ball in the corners of the opponent's service court 70 percent of the time, the chances for success are greatly enhanced. If spin, with accuracy, can be applied to the ball during service, a variety of serves can be used to confuse the receiver. In addition, the server can capitalize on the receiver's weakness in returning a serve if those weaknesses can be recognized (Figure 9.3).

Figure 9.3   Service and service return position.

Placement of Service Strategy

Placement of the service should be deep (Figure 9.4). Then choices can be made as to where the ball should be directed to cause the most problems for the receiver. If the receiver is right-handed and has a weak backhand, the left corner of the left service court might be advantageous to the server (Figure 9.5). If the receiver moves to the left to protect against returning a backhand, the server can place the next serve to the right of both service courts out of the reach of the receiver. If a server has a reasonable velocity on a flat serve, the receiver will have problems if the ball is placed directly in front of the body, particularly if the player is tall or slow. A slice serve can be hit wide to the right side of the right service court, pulling the receiver off the court and consequently opening the whole court for the next shot by the server (Figure 9.6).

A slice service to the right corner of the left service court pulls the receiver to the middle of the court, causing a down-the-middle return (Figure 9.7).

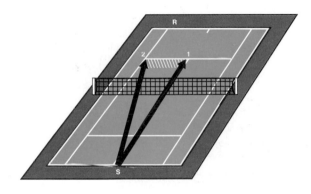

Figure 9.4   Hitting deep serves.

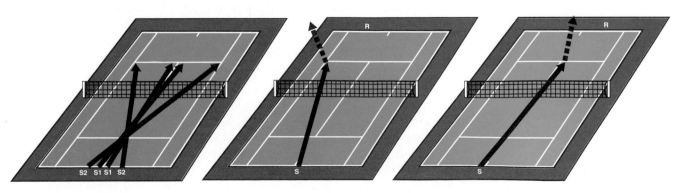

Figure 9.5   Hitting the corners on the serve.

Figure 9.6   Placing slice serves.

Figure 9.7   Placing slice serves to the left service court.

The Second Service Strategy

The second service is even more important in the sense that if it is not accurately placed in the appropriate service court, the point is lost without a response from the receiver. The second serve not only must be reliable and accurate, but should have some pace associated with the stroke. Many servers make the mistake of pushing the ball into the service court rather than hitting with good form. The three points required for a sound second serve are: 1) the serve must have accuracy coupled with pace, 2) the serve must have spin to insure accuracy, and 3) the serve must never be pushed or blooped into the service court. Accuracy is enhanced by a slice or service with some attention to placement of the ball and pace.

Return of Service Strategy

Return of service is a crucial part of strategy. The server's role is to place the ball in play, and the return player's role is to keep the ball in play. The strategy is to hit the ball back with pace, and to hit it deep to eliminate the initial advantage of the server. The server who relies on the serve to win points will begin to lose confidence if the ball keeps coming back.

There is a cause-effect relationship which implies that the receiver should respond to the server's pace and depth of serve by standing beyond the baseline to return serve. Part of understanding strategy is to dispel such thought.

If the server has a strong spin, it is best to step inside the baseline and cut down the sidespin or high bounce before the effect can occur. A serve that is pushed over the net should be returned firmly and deeply, and the receiver should avoid the tendency to "kill" the ball. The receiver can use various placements when returning the serve that will enhance the play at that point. Returning *down the line* is usually a mistake when the server stays on the baseline. A shot down the line will leave the court open for a cross-court winner by the server. Service returns are most effective when hit back along the line of flight of the serve, and when hit at the feet of the server. When serves are hit with little pace, the receiver has more options, including down the line, cross-court, and angled cross-court. The effort off a weak serve should be to hit a winner under control, forcing the opposing server to hit while moving to the ball, or to miss the ball entirely (Figure 9.8).

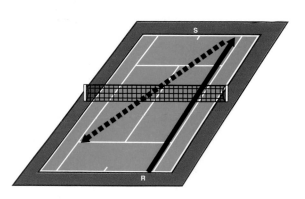

Figure 9.8 Return of serve down the line consequences.

ATTACKING THE NET AND BEATING THE NET PLAYER

Judgments that must be made by a player include when to go to the net, and, once there, when to stay and when to leave. There are three situations in which a player should go to the net: 1) off a serve, 2) off an approach shot, and 3) off a firmly hit groundstroke that forces the opponent to move behind the baseline when returning the shot. When at the net, there are two times to stay and continue play at the net: 1) when following one volley with another, and 2) when hitting an overhead smash from between the service court line and the net. Retreat occurs in only one situation — when a lob is hit deep to the baseline, compelling the net player to leave the net to return the lob. The player attacking the net should apply the *Division Line Theory* by following the path of the ball to the net, consequently dividing the court in half between the two players. The division line will enable the net player to cover all territory equally between the forehand and backhand and give the opponent only one possible winning shot. If, as an example, the net player hits to the deep, right baseline corner of the opponent and takes a step and a half to the left of the center of the net, the only possible return for a winning shot is to the far right corner angled at the net (Figure 9.9).

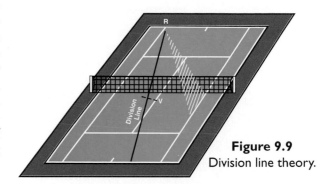

Figure 9.9
Division line theory.

Going To The Net Strategy

Going to the net following a serve suggests the execution of an accurate serve. A serve with pace provides the opportunity to go to the net, since the return of serve may be weak, but the high velocity eliminates deep penetration to the net by the server (Figure 9.10). If a server can get to the service court line when following a paced serve, then penetration is as close as it is going to be. If the return of serve is a miss hit, the server can pounce on the return with an effective volley twenty feet from the net. If the return of serve is at the feet of the server, who has advanced on the net, a twenty-foot return distance from the net may become a liability. The server now has to be an exceptional volleyer, since the ball at the feet creates vulnerability. A slice service permits

Figure 9.10   Server going to the net.

the player to advance closer to the net before being forced to stop and respond to the opponent's return of serve (Figure 9.11).

Going to the net following an approach shot is an ideal time to advance on the net. If the return from the opponent is short — at the service line in the middle of the court — the approach shot can be played to the corners. Once the ball is hit to the corner, the player advances to the net, in line with the ball, and volleys cross-court (Figure 9.12). If a return shot is hit to the service line, close to and parallel to a sideline, the approach shot should be down the sideline followed by a short angled volley cross-court as the player advances on to the net (Figure 9.13).

Going to the net off a groundstroke must be done with some prudence. It is inadvisable to go to the net when the groundstroke 1) has not been hit with authority, 2) has not been hit deep to the baseline, and 3) has not forced the opponent to return the shot while moving away from the net. However, if the player has hit an effective groundstroke, then that player must learn to *close in on the net*. As the player advances to the net from the baseline, a ready position must be assumed prior to the return shot crossing the net. Once a return has been hit by the advancing player, that player continues on to the net in a line with the ball, and again stops in a ready position before the return shot crosses the net. It takes between two and three stops to gain control of the net and be in control of hitting

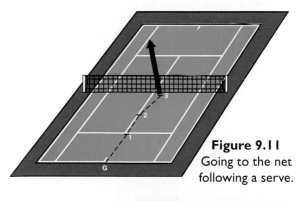

Figure 9.11
Going to the net
following a serve.

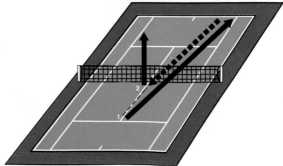

Figure 9.12   Going to the net following an approach shot from the middle of the court.

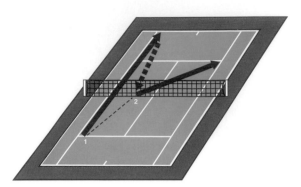

Figure 9.13 Going to the net following an approach shot from the sideline area of the court.

a winning shot if the opponent is able to respond with some degree of authority in returning the shots hit by the advancing player. Three thoughts should be on the mind of the player advancing from the baseline: 1) volley and advance, 2) punch the ball deep to the baseline, and 3) hit at the feet of the opponent so that the return is "up."

Advancing to the net is an adventure and a reward if the end result is a winning shot. The choice of going to the net is made based on the advantage that it will give the player to advance. There are some final thoughts associated with attacking the net. First, the volleyer must always stop and assume a ready position prior to the return shot crossing the net. Second, when attacking, the player should follow the path of the ball to provide the division line. A third thought is to get close to the net to hit a volley. A beginning player needs to be a racket and a half length away from the net, while a skilled player can volley from the service court line. All players who volley must remember to stay low and punch the ball.

Beating The Net Player Strategy

There is a *threefold strategy to beat the player who attacks the net:* 1) hit at the feet of the net player, 2) hit a passing shot, and 3) hit a lob.

Hitting at the feet of the net player forces the player to hit the ball up in the air, providing a set up to hit a winning return. Two shots are most often used to hit at the feet of a player at the net. A topspin stroke is usually hit from the baseline to the feet of a player at the net, and from a serve, a ball is often blocked back to the feet of an advancing net player.

Hitting a passing shot to beat a net player is a second means of defeating the volleyer at the net. The passing shot may be hit down the line or as a short-angled cross-court shot. As an example, if a player is to the left of the center mark at the baseline, a shot down the net player's right sideline could pass that player. A ball hit further to the left of the baseline player can be played as a short-angled cross-court passing shot, since the net player has moved to the right of center to establish the division line (Figure 9.14).

The third method of *beating the net player is with a lob*. A net player tends to get too close to the net to avoid hitting balls at the feet. When this happens, the ability to retreat and cover a deep lob is diminished, and the player at the baseline has a clear-cut choice of hitting an offensive, topspin lob to the net player's baseline. If the players are beginners, any form of a lob that gets over the head of the net player will be effective. The important point is to drive the opponent back from the net, insuring a return on the move with the back to the net.

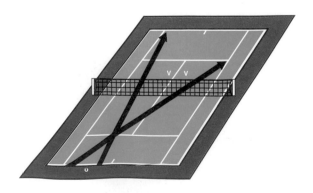

Figure 9.14 Hitting a passing shot to beat a net player.

LOB AND OVERHEAD SMASH STRATEGY

Lobs and overhead smashes are an integral part of overall court strategy. The lob can be both a defensive and offensive shot, and the overhead smash is a reward for effective serve or groundstroke play.

Lob Strategy

Hitting lobs as both offensive and defensive shots is an important part of strategy. The question in singles play is *when to hit a lob, and what kind to hit.* Defensive lobs should be hit whenever the opponent has forced the play, and whenever a player needs to "buy time" to recover from a strong shot. The important part of a defensive lob is to hit to the opponent's backhand, forcing the opponent to run around the ball to hit an overhead smash, or to return the ball going away from the net with a backhand stroke. There is a particular way to chase a lob for a return that helps a player to recover from a lob more readily. When retrieving a lob, the player, instead of running in a straight line, should run to the outside of the ball and come from behind it to either hit a return lob, a forceful groundstroke, or an overhead smash (Figure 9.15). A lob that has the effect of an offensive shot should, of course, be hit when the opposing net player is too close to the net.

Figure 9.15   Retrieving a lob.

Overhead Smash Strategy

Overhead smashes are used in singles strategy to respond to lobs that are hit between the service court and the net (Figure 9.16). Setting up is an important part of that strategy. A crisp volley down the opponent's right sideline forces that player to execute a lob that travels to the middle of the court, which, in turn, can be hit as an overhead smash to the opponent's left corner (Figure 9.17). This example illustrates that a firm offensive shot creates a weak lob return, and for each lob return, there are a large variety of targets for the overhead smash. Balls hit deep to the opponent's baseline are always acceptable as effective overheads (Figure 9.18). When the return lob is closer to

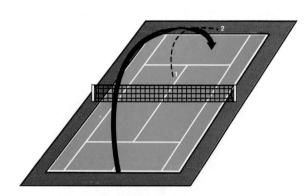

Figure 9.16   Overhead smash set up.

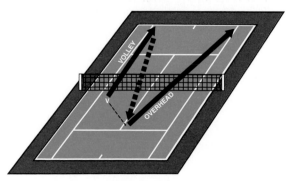

Figure 9.17   Setting up an overhead return with a volley shot.

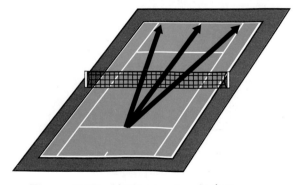

Figure 9.18   Hitting overheads deep.

the net, smashes can be angled and bounced out of the opponent's court (Figure 9.19). The angle and bounce carry the ball into a non-returnable location. Angles and deeply angled overhead smashes are also effective. They insure that the opponent has to move to retrieve the overhead, rather than remain stationary and hit a lob with control. An angled overhead is an excellent placement for a backhand overhead, since it is more important to be accurate in placement rather than fast for successful completion of the shot (Figure 9.20).

Often the first overhead smash is not a winning shot, nor should it be expected to be. The first overhead "softens" up the opponent, who can only return the shot from a defensive position. Strategywise, if the player hitting the lob keeps the overhead consistently deep and angled, the opponent returning lobs eventually wears down, or breaks down skillwise, and hits a short lob that can be returned as a winning overhead.

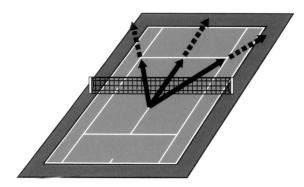

Figure 9.19   Hitting angled overhead smashes.

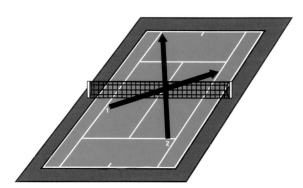

Figure 9.20   Angled and deeply angled overhead smashes.

BASELINE PLAY STRATEGY

Figure 9.21   Baseline play set up.

Baseline play involves giving complete, undivided attention to hitting groundstrokes deep, and relying on percentage tennis to its fullest. The idea is to force the opponent to make a mistake with a miss hit shot or poorly hit return. There are several ways of forcing an error from the opponent, including cross-court and down-the-line shots (Figure 9.21).

Duplicating The Opponent's Groundstroke Return Strategy

Duplicating the opponent's return is good strategy because it puts pressure on the opponent to change the direction of the ball. Singles strategy dictates that if the opponent hits cross-court the player should return cross-court until the opponent hits down the line. At that point, the player has the option of returning in duplication down the line or coming back cross-court. In either case, the advantage is with the player as opposed to the opponent, since the return angle favors the player's stroke, and because there is an element of the unknown in the return direction (Figure 9.22).

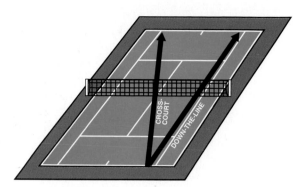

Figure 9.22   Duplication groundstroke returns.

Moving The Opponent Strategy

Another type of strategy is to move the opponent back and forth across the baseline, forcing alternate forehand and backhand returns. If the opponent can be driven from one side of the court to the other, reaching for shot returns, eventually the ball will be returned short or "up" so that an approach shot, volley, or overhead can be used as a follow-up to good baseline play. With skill and experience, the baseline player can develop strategy using varied strokes, always coming back to hit with depth and angle that will cause the opponent to make a mistake. Sometimes varying the stroke is disguised by hitting down that sideline with a groundstroke to the opponent's backhand for a succession of shots, then switching to a cross-court shot that pulls the opponent out of a groove and requires a totally new stroke in the rally. Hitting the groundstroke over and over again to the same side will also wear down an opponent's confidence, and the skill of the stroke will weaken as the belief in winning the point lessens.

Scoring Situation Strategy

There are *certain scoring situations* in a match that are vital to good strategy and success. In a game, a score of 30-15 is important. If the next point is won, the score will be 40-15, and there is a two-point difference for the leading player to use to an advantage. If the 30-15 score becomes 30-30, either player may win the next two points. A set score of 5-3 with the opponent serving is a crucial situation in the ninth game. If the opponent wins that game, the set is over at a 6-3 score. If the receiver of serve wins the ninth game, the score becomes 4-5, and the player who is behind serves with a tie set possible at 5-5 in the tenth game. Obviously, the 4-5 set score is also important, but the player behind is serving, and with a degree of serving skill, the server has the advantage. Other scores that are meaningful are the first point of any given game, or the last point of a game, set, or match.

Game Plan Strategy

The *overall game strategy and plan* are only as good as the skill of the player. The game plan for an early beginner is to do the best possible to return shots back across the net. By the time the player can hit with some consistency, percentage tennis really becomes important. It means that the advanced beginner can work at hitting the ball back with depth and patience and begin to set up an opponent with subtle techniques to force an error. Continual maturation permits the player to understand that the mind is the most important part of the game. The ability to out-think the opponent becomes the key to victory. Changing pace, moving a player along the baseline, and moving the opponent to the net and back away from the net all begin to make sense.

The game plan and strategy for a player start with the warm-up and end with the last point of the match. In the warm-up, the player begins to assess the opponent's ability, being careful not to become overly confident of or intimidated by the opponent. During the warm-up, each player should determine the skills of the opponent and what strokes that opponent is capable of hitting effectively. It should be cautioned that the player who is assessing should not change the game plan only to meet the opponent's skills. The assessing player must be able to react in a normal manner and not play as the opponent dictates. An example of a game plan is that if the opponent likes to serve and volley, the strategy would be to prepare to hit passing shots, lobs, and groundstrokes at the opponent's feet. Another example would be to stay at home base during a rally and force the opponent to rally from the baseline when the opponent lacks consistency in hitting groundstrokes. Game plans and strategy should be a combination of the player reacting to the opponent's weaknesses, and playing to the level of skills possessed.

Final game strategy thoughts include playing every point and returning every shot. Second, look for the short ball, and attack with an aggressive approach shot, completing the attack by continuing on to the net. Third, be consistent in play rather than hit the one spectacular shot. Fourth, remember that defensive lobs "buy time" and that most tennis players cannot hit solid overheads in reacting to a lob. Finally, if a player will keep all groundstrokes in play and deep, and hit all serves with pace and accuracy, the possibilities for success increase greatly.

Doubles Strategy

10

Doubles strategy is entirely different from singles strategy with the exception of the strokes that are used. Doubles is an attacking game; singles tends to be a more passive defensive game. Doubles play is located at the net or retreating from the net, while singles play is positioned at the baseline. The attacking concept of doubles provides an exciting type of match filled with shots executed quickly and with good reactions. The beginner seldom experiences the challenge of the game, yet this is the first type of situation that a beginner may face if being taught in a college class or in any group, since only a few courts are available for a large instructional group. The beginning player can get a sense of playing doubles and begin to develop the attacking skills necessary for success.

BASIC ALIGNMENTS AND FORMATIONS

There are numerous formations related to doubles play, including club or recreational social doubles (usually college class doubles), conventional doubles, mixed doubles, and Australian doubles. Choosing a partner and deciding where each partner will be aligned on the court is part of good strategy in that individual skills can be used to the advantage of a team.

Two-Back Formation

The beginning player should start from one of two formations, depending on how advanced the players are in executing strokes. These formations are associated with *social doubles*. If the players have yet to be introduced to net play, including volleying and overhead smashes, it is best to begin doubles at the baseline in a two-back formation.

The *two-back formation* is also used by experienced players when the opposing team is at the net hitting overhead smashes while the two on the baseline team attempt to return lobs to defend against the overheads (Figure 10.1). The weakness of the two-back formation is the defensive stature of the team and their lack of control at the net. A team that controls the net has an open court that will allow large areas in which to place the ball for winning shots. From the baseline, shots hit at players controlling the net have little potential for success because they involve only small target areas that cannot be covered at the net by the two players (Figure 10.2).

The bottom line is: It is ridiculous to place players at the net who do not have the skill to protect themselves or to hit a volley or overhead smash.

Figure 10.1　Two-back formation.

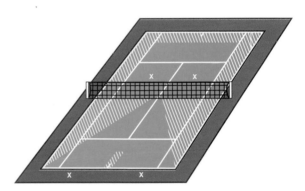

Figure 10.2　Target areas for two-up versus two-back.

Figure 10.3　One-up one-back formation (serving).

One-Up One-Back Formation

A second formation is *one up and one back*. This alignment is used when the players net experience is at least adequate for protection at the net, and for execution of firmly hit volleys (Figure 10.3).

One player up and one player back occurs due to the original alignment of the players in the serving positions. The problem occurs when the server doesn't have the confidence to serve and follow the serve to the net, or the return player does not follow the return to the net. Once the alignment holds at one-up one-back, that alignment becomes vulnerable to open area winning shots. (See Figures 10.4–10.5)

Figure 10.4   One-up, one-back formation (receiving).

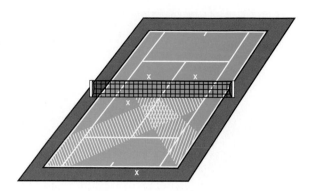

Figure 10.5   Target areas for two-up against one-up one-back.

Conventional Doubles Formation: Two-Up in Tandem

Conventional doubles requires that a team attack the net, and, if need be, attack face to face with the opposing team. The key to good doubles play is to work together in a tandem. If the ball is lobbed deep when the team is at the net, they must retreat together, and when one player hits an overhead smash from the service court line, they both must advance to the net together. Playing conventional doubles is working as a team, knowing where the other player is located, and depending on the partner to hit the appropriate shot. When controlling the net, the doubles team attacks side by side, positioning themselves in the middle of the two service courts. From that position, as if they were on a string, they move up and back and side to side in a balanced position (Figure 10.6).

There are a significant number of movement patterns on the court from a conventional formation. First, a teammate may *poach* in doubles. The definition is important. The poach is hitting a winning volley; there is no margin for error. The net player steps across parallel to the net to hit a volley directed toward the partner at the baseline following a serve. The serving partner sees the poach attempt and veers to replace the position vacated by the poaching partner (Figure 10.7).

Another team movement pattern is to retreat to hit a lob, then recover for the next shot. The retreat incorporates a cross-action by team members to reach the ball. If the lob is to the left deep corner of the baseline, the partner on the right can see the ball and react to it better than the partner who would have to retreat in a straight line with the back to the opponents. At this

Figure 10.6   Two-up formation (conventional doubles).

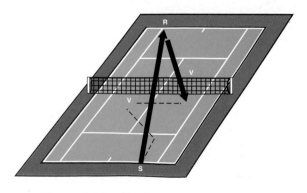

Figure 10.7   Poach movement patterns.

Figure 10.8   Retreat to return a lob (cross action).

point, the partners are now at the baseline where they will remain in a defensive posture until they can regain an advantage and return to the net (Figures 10.8 and 10.9).

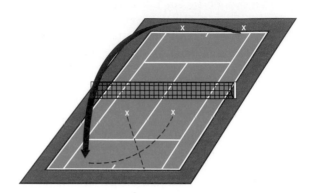

Figure 10.9   Movement pattern for retreating to return a lob.

Conventional Doubles Formation: Mixed Doubles

Mixed doubles is a combination of one male and one female partner, and the formation used is the same as for conventional doubles. The only real change is related to the physical strength of the female partner. If there is a strength difference (the strength difference could also be found between 2 male or 2 female partners), the alignment may have to be adjusted. The reality of mixed doubles is that typically the female is attacked as often as possible by the opposing team. When a female player serves to a female opponent, the male at the net must poach whenever possible. With the female serving, the velocity or pace of the serve is not usually as great as when the male partner serves; consequently, the female server must stay in an up-back alignment. That alignment has already been identified as a weak formation, and it is the reason for the male partner poaching. A serve to the backhand of the return player will aid the serving team by making it easier to poach by the male partner, and easier for the female partner to respond to a groundstroke return.

When receiving against the female server, several responses can be made. One may be a direct return back to the male net player. If successful, the male partner will eventually retreat to the baseline to avoid being hit by a return of serve. A second strategy is to return serve cross-court. This subjects the server to returning a groundstroke from a defensive position, and avoids the male partner at the net.

Mixed doubles is a delightful game, and it can be highly competitive. Each partner has a role to play and a responsibility to fulfill. Strategy for mixed doubles can be enlarged to cover any doubles where the characteristics are similar. If one partner is a physically stronger partner but the players are of the same sex, the same approach to strategy should be used.

Special Formations

There is also a service formation that can help a team in special situations.

Australian Doubles

Australian Doubles eliminates an opposing team's cross-court return. The alignment is the serve and net player situated in a perpendicular line to the net with both players on the same side of the server's court. If the server is serving to the opposing team's right service court, the server will be to the right of the center mark, and the net partner will be set up on the inside center of the serving team's right service court (Figure 10.10). This alignment leaves the left service court of the serving team open during the serve. Following the serve, the baseline server moves to the left to cover the open court from the baseline. The partner at the net stays to create an up-back situation (Figure 10.11).

There are several options with the Australian formation. The first is for the net player to cross to the left service court following the serve, while the serving partner moves further to the right side of the baseline to protect that side of the court. A second option is for the team to crisscross following the serve, with the net player moving to the left and the server going straight to the net from the right side. A variation of the crisscross would be for the server to follow the serve to the net on the left side, with the net player staying in the same position.

The more variations the Australian doubles formation can offer to the opposing team, the more confused they can become, and the more chance for success. This formation is ideal for the team with one weak serving partner or a team with one partner who has a major skill weakness that can be hidden by the alignment.

I Formation

Another special service formation is called an I Formation. It is also a formation that positions the net player at the net, straddling the middle service court line. It's strength is down the middle, and if the server serves wide, forcing a cross court return, the net player is positioned to respond with a potential winning volley. In fact, any serve that forces a return down the middle is advantageous to the doubles serving team, but there is also a vulnerability that permits the receiving team to hit shots down the lines for winners.

The I Formation gives the receiving team a "different look" from the serving team and forces them to make adjustments. Sometimes even a small adjustment creates mistakes by the team that is doing the adjusting, and works to the advantage of the more creative I-Formation team (Figure 10.12).

Figure 10.10 Australian doubles formation.

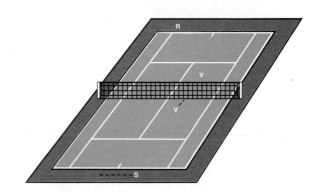

Figure 10.11 Movement pattern for Australian doubles formation.

Figure 10.12 I Formation.

SERVICE AND RETURN OF SERVICE STRATEGY

Doubles play strategy is based on effective service and return of service. In addition, the full enjoyment of doubles play is realized when players are consistent in executing serves and return of service.

Service Strategy

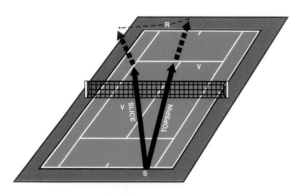

Figure 10.13   First serve targets.

The first service in doubles is of extreme importance. Three-fourths of all first serves should be hit successfully to give the serving team the leverage of moving to the net as a team in a two-up volley situation. Once the developing player has progressed beyond hitting flat services with pace to areas of the opponent's service courts, spin serves should be used in the majority of situations.

A slice serve should be used when serving to the opposing team's right service court to force the receiver off the court, and to allow the attacking serving team to overplay to their left to control the net. To reiterate, the service must be consistently accurate, and the placement, with spin, must be thoughtfully considered (Figure 10.13). Additionally, the beginner must work hard at protecting the partner at the net during service. A soft, pushed serve will endanger that partner and compel the team to play two back on the serve, thus defeating the advantage of controlling the net by the serving team.

Return of Service Strategy

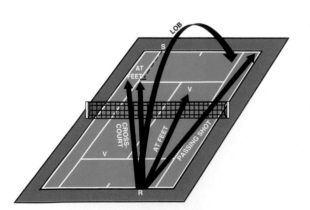

Figure 10.14   Options for return of service in doubles.

There are two considerations attached to a *return of service* in doubles: first, to get the ball back over the net at the serving team's feet; second, to select the best target placement of the return, and then complete that task. The first consideration is an obvious strategy related to self-preservation that has to be the prerequisite with no exceptions. The second consideration requires more planning and assessment of at least four options for target areas (Figure 10.14):

1. Return the ball to the feet of the net player or the advancing server.
2. Pass the net player.
3. Lob the net player.
4. Hit cross-court angled toward the server.

The first three options were discussed in an earlier chapter as they related to playing a net player. With a service return, lobbing becomes difficult with a serve of any pace, but it is reasonably effective off a soft serve. If the net player does not advance on the net to within two steps from net position, the return at the net player can be effective also.

Passing the net player requires that the player at the net lean to the middle with anticipation of poaching, and the return is directed toward the alley. Being able to pass an opponent at the net down the alley is a demoralizing act, since that is the one area the net player must protect.

The angled cross-court returns and cross-court returns at the on-rushing server's feet are exceptional for hitting winning shots. Angled cross-court shots cannot be reached by the server unless the server anticipates the shot, or the angled return lacks crispness. Cross-court shots at the feet of the server moving to the net catch the server in a tentative position, and the final result is often a ball hit up for an easy volley by the receiving team.

The choice of which return to hit is to a large extent controlled by the placement of the serve in the service court, and by the velocity of the serve. A serve hit to the inside corner of the right service court usually eliminates the passing shot at the net player due to the central location of the ball. All other service returns from that location remain possible, with the best choice a return at the attacking server's feet. A serve placement to the inside of the left service court has the same response as the serve to the inside of the right service court. Serves hit wide to the respective service courts permit all four service return options to be used.

The major lesson to be learned is that a good server will only give the receiver a limited number of options to select from during any given service situation. If a serve is well placed, the receiver will return serve to anticipated areas on the serving team's side of the court. One last consideration of return of serve is for the receiving player to always get the racket on the ball. All strategy for a return of serve collapses if the receiver misses the return.

THE DOUBLES GAME PLAN AND STRATEGY

The doubles plan of strategy is to execute strokes in an attacking manner working to gain control of the net. All players at all levels of skill must do these two things. One of the easier skills in tennis is the volley shot. If a beginner can get to the net, play will be highly enjoyable from that position. Once the concept of taking control of the net is ingrained, the doubles team must remember to protect the alley and middle of the court. They must learn to move as a team, in tandem, supporting each other and retreating or advancing together. The receiving team must return serves on a low trajectory with pace and attempt to hit a predetermined target area. The serving team needs to establish a relentless plan of attack with the server coming to the net following a well-paced serve. The final plan is to communicate with the partner, out-think the opposing team, and out-reach the opponent.

Tennis Practice By Yourself and With A Partner

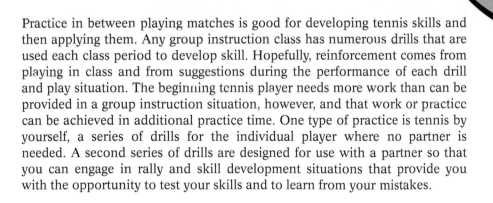

Practice in between playing matches is good for developing tennis skills and then applying them. Any group instruction class has numerous drills that are used each class period to develop skill. Hopefully, reinforcement comes from playing in class and from suggestions during the performance of each drill and play situation. The beginning tennis player needs more work than can be provided in a group instruction situation, however, and that work or practice can be achieved in additional practice time. One type of practice is tennis by yourself, a series of drills for the individual player where no partner is needed. A second series of drills are designed for use with a partner so that you can engage in rally and skill development situations that provide you with the opportunity to test your skills and to learn from your mistakes.

TENNIS BY YOURSELF

Tennis by yourself involves drills that require no partner, develops strokes with a checkpoint of mechanics reminders, and encourages variation in the drill selection. There are many occasions when a player cannot find a suitable partner or one who wants to practice. The drills presented below will take 45 minutes and will give the beginning player a good physical workout plus a skill practice session that requires only one participant.

Serving Practice Drill

The *serving* practice drill requires a player to use thirty tennis balls in serving to targets. The level of skill will establish the type of serves hit, and through a series of six sets, a player will hit 180 tennis serves.

Set #1

Serve 30 balls to the left service court — inside corner.

Set #2:

Serve 30 balls to the right service court — inside corner.

Set #3:

Serve 30 balls to the left service court — outside corner.

Set #4:

Serve 30 balls to the right service court — outside corner.

Set #5:

Serve 30 balls to the left service court — 10 to the outside, 10 to the middle, 10 to the inside.

Set #6:

Serve 30 balls to the right service court — 10 to the outside, 10 to the middle, 10 to the inside.

Movement Requirement

Player must run to the other side of the court and retrieve balls in a pickup run fashion.

Variations

Variations are quite acceptable, but only one type of serve per set should be initiated. A good variation is to serve and to go to the net for a volley, stopping as the ball strikes the service court.

CHECKPOINT OF MECHANICS

Counting successful serves might be insightful, but total concentration on mechanics will be more productive.

1. Am I looking at the tennis ball on the toss?
2. Is my toss accurate? high enough? in line?
3. Are my feet where they belong?
4. Do I have a full back swing? follow through?
5. Is my grip appropriate to my serve?
6. Am I accurate? why? why not?

Groundstroke Drill

The second drill — a simple *groundstroke* — uses a wall board, but goals must be set through the sequence. There are nine sets in the drill lasting sixty seconds each. After each stroke, the player must return to ready position and allow a distance to permit the ball to bounce twice before each stroke.

Set #1

Hit repetitive forehands.

Set #2

Hit repetitive backhands (remember to selfdrop on the backhand side).

Set #3

Alternate forehand and backhand.

Sets #4, 5, and 6

Repeat sets 1-3 with slice.

Sets #7, 8, and 9

Repeat sets 1-3 with topspin.

CHECKPOINT OF MECHANICS

1. Am I looking the ball into the racket?
2. Am I transferring weight into the ball?
3. Do I have a full back swing? follow through?
4. Am I hitting with the appropriate grip?
5. Am I turning my shoulder early?
6. Is the ball at least 5' high on the wall board?
7. Am I accurate? why? why not?

Approach Shot Drill

The third drill is designed to develop confidence and eliminate overanxiety in players hitting *approach shots*. Approach shots are seldom executed in practice, so hitting four sets of thirty balls each will provide a good mental inset. Aim at the service court line for depth and 4' in from the sideline for accuracy. The player should drop the balls at least 2 feet away and at least waist high.

Set #1

From middle of the right service court, hit forehand down the line.

Set #2

From middle of the left service court, hit backhand down the line.

Set #3

From middle of the right service court, hit forehand cross-court.

Set #4

From middle of the left service court, hit backhand cross-court.

Movement Requirement

Player must run to the other side of the court and retrieve balls in a pickup run fashion (Figure 11.1).

Variations

The type of shot can be varied. The basic ground-stroke pattern can be used, but as topspin and slice strokes are developed they should be incorporated in the drill. Hitting topspin down the line is another variation of the drill. Also, placing the ball on the drop in different areas of the service court and between the baseline and the service court line contributes to variation.

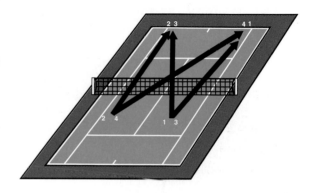

Figure 11.1   Approach shot movement drill.

CHECKPOINT OF MECHANICS

1. Am I letting the ball drop, and am I timing my strokes?
2. Am I looking the ball into my racket?
3. Am I transferring my weight?
4. Is my backswing shortened?
5. Am I hitting into the court? why? why not?

Moving Drill

Moving is a prime need for a tennis player. Coupled with agility and quickness, movement can aid the player in getting to the ball in time. Three sets are designed to encourage agility and quickness and use of the racket in shadow boxing.

Set #1

The player should move to imaginary numbers and, in sequence, shadow box either a groundstroke, approach shot, or volley. All balls stroked up to the service line require the players to return to ready position on the baseline, and all balls between the service line and the net require the player to assume a ready position at the net in the middle (Figure 11.2).

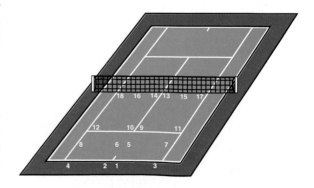

Figure 11.2   Shadow boxing movement, Set #1.

Set #2

The same drill as above except the shadow boxing should consist of lobs from the baseline and overhead smashes from the net. Player must assume ready position on each stroke (Figure 11.3).

Set #3

The player eliminates shadow boxing and moves along the lines of the court, touching each junction between two lines (Figure 11.4).

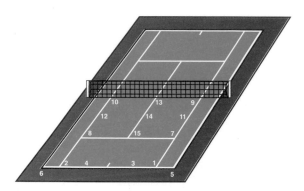

Figure 11.3   Shadow boxing movement, Set #2.

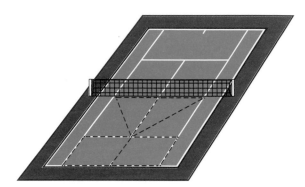

Figure 11.4   Fitness movement drill, Set #3.

Overhead Smash Drill

The final drill is an *overhead smash*. The exercise requires a simple bounce of the ball off the court and above the head, providing time for the player to get set underneath the ball and hit an overhead smash.

Set #1

Hit 15 overheads from the right middle service court.

Set #2

Hit 15 overheads from the left middle service court.

Set #3

Hit 15 overheads from the right center position halfway between baseline and service line.

Set #4

Hit 15 overheads from the left center position halfway between baseline and service line.

Movement Requirement

After each pair of sets, the player must run to the other side of the court and retrieve balls in a pickup fashion.

Variations

The player may locate other spots to hit the overhead and begin to identify the location of the target on the other side of the court.

CHECKPOINT OF MECHANICS

1. Am I timing my stroke in a smooth, rhythmical motion?

2. Is my backswing in the middle of my shoulder blades and my elbow up at a right angle?

3. Do I have my non-racket hand pointing in reference to the ball?

4. Am I hitting into the court? why? why not?

There are numerous sets for each skill and other skills that can be developed. The key to executing the drills is having a little self-discipline, becoming goal oriented, and building confidence that each skill can be performed. If the beginning player will participate three times per week in "tennis by yourself," a marked change in skill development will occur.

PARTNER PRACTICE DRILLS

Partner practice drills supplement what you can practice on your own. There are countless numbers of drills that involve two players. Eleven drills are presented in this chapter to provide a beginning approach to practice. Five of the drills are groundstroke oriented because groundstrokes are the base for the game. There are also drills to reinforce lobs, overheads, volley shots, and attacking the net.

Groundstroke Drills

Groundstroke drills progress from simple to fairly complicated.

Short Court Drills

The short court drill is a "touch" drill that requires the partners to stand in the service court of their respective side and hit groundstrokes with touch (Figure 11.5). The idea is to keep the ball within the confines of the service court and to assist the player in anticipation, shoulder turn, and sensing the "feel" of the stroke.

Bounce/Hit Drill

The bounce/hit drill is designed to encourage focus and an inner feel for the groundstroke (Figure 11.6). The idea is for the partners to hit the ball from baseline to baseline without thinking about the mechanics of the stroke. By verbally shouting "bounce" every time the ball bounces on the court and "hit" every time the ball is hit, the partners begin to focus on the ball and concentrate on the end result of hitting the ball to the other side of the court.

What is amazing is that form and mechanics of the groundstroke surface naturally when the partners really become involved in the drill. There are two points to remember when executing this drill. First, "bounce" and "hit" must be identified by both partners regardless of which side of the net the ball is on. Second, the verbal response must be loud enough for both partners to hear. There is a tendency to be self-conscious when doing this drill, and if there are players on adjacent courts, the etiquette of quiet on the courts might be breached. But the drill, used properly, will truly be of help in skill development.

Figure 11.5 Short court drill.

Figure 11.6 Bounce/hit drill.

Figure 11.7   Down-the-line groundstroke drill.

Figure 11.8   Cross-court groundstroke drill.

Down-the-Line Groundstrokes

Hitting down-the-line groundstrokes encourage establishing a target when hitting the ball (Figure 11.7). The idea is to hit the ball down the sideline to the other partner. The ball should be positioned so that the ball is between the player and the sideline, forcing the player to hit a forehand or backhand, depending on which is the appropriate shot (e.g., with two right-handed players one would be hitting with a forehand, the other with a backhand groundstroke). After hitting the ball, the player that has just hit returns to near the baseline center mark area. The idea is to have to move to hit the ball with the appropriate groundstroke rather than standing in one spot and eventually playing the ball so it is positioned for a choice of a forehand or backhand.

Cross-Court Groundstroke

The cross court groundstroke drill has the same purpose of setting a target and the same organizational setup, but instead of going down the line the ball is hit cross-court (Figure 11.8). Again, it is important to hit the ball and return to near the center mark. For beginners, these last two drills are somewhat difficult. There is a frustration level because you might be uncomfortable with hitting a backhand and reaching the intended target. It is important, however, to increase skill level because you will not improve if you don't push yourself.

Down-the-Line/Cross-Court

The final groundstroke drill adds to the difficulty progression because it combines *down-the-line with cross-court*. The idea follows the sequence of: 1) Partner A hitting down the left sideline, 2) Partner B returning a cross-court shot to the right side court of Partner A, 3) Partner A then hitting down the right sideline to Partner B who returns a shot cross-court to Partner A's left side court. (See Figures 11.9–11.12.) The sequence repeats itself for development of consistency.

Figure 11.9   Partner A hits down the left sideline.

Figure 11.10   Partner B returns a cross-court shot to the right side court of Partner A.

Figure 11.11   Partner A hits down the right sideline to Partner B.

Figure 11.12   Partner B returns a shot cross-court to Partner A's left side court.

Lob Drills

Two partner drills incorporate first a lob sequence followed by a lob/overhead smash sequence.

Lob Sequence

The *lob drill* simply requires the partners to exchange lobs (Figure 11.13). An emphasis should be made on hitting deep with proper height for the selected lob. You should start with a defensive lob and experiment with ball height, and then continue by hitting topspin offensive lobs. Work on an equal number of forehand and backhand lobs, and as you progress you should begin to place the lobs from corner to corner.

Figure 11.13   Lob drill.

Figure 11.14   Overhead smash sequence drill.

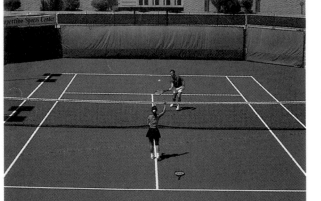

Figure 11.15   Toss/Volley drill.

Figure 11.16   Face-to-face volley drill.

Lob Drill/Overhead Smash Sequence

The second drill is an extension of the lob drill. It includes an *overhead smash at the end of the lob* with one partner self-dropping and lobbing short to their service court area and the other partner hitting overheads (Figure 11.14). As you improve, it is important to work on returning an overhead with a lob rather than self-dropping to initiate the overhead shot of the partner.

Volley Drills

There are two volley drills that enhance skill of all players, including beginners: the *toss/volley drill* and the *face-to-face volley*.

Toss/Volley Drill

The toss/volley drill requires that one partner toss the ball to the other partner. (Figure 11.15) The idea is to toss accurately to force the volleying partner to step into the ball with a short backswing and punch the ball back to the partner. This drill encourages good form, and it can progress with variations that force the volleying partner to hit low and high volleys plus adjusting to a ball at the body. In addition, the toss of the partner can force the volleying partner to cross-step and punch the ball deep to the baseline.

Face-To-Face Volley

This volley drill is a particularly fun drill because both partners face each other within their service courts and volley the ball back and forth (Figure 11.16). Progression is again important. Start with forehand to forehand volleys, then volley backhand to backhand. As your skill increases you can then alternate from forehand to backhand volleys, hit volleys at different elevations of the ball, and react to each placement of the ball that comes to you.

Service Returns

Service returns are seldom practiced and as a result returns are neglected. The drill is simple; one partner serves, the other returns the serve (Figure 11.17). Focus on returns should be a first priority to hit them back deep to the baseline. Then service returns can become more target oriented

Figure 11.17   Service return drill.

by hitting both cross-court and down-the-line returns. To really become skilled in return of service, the return partner should have the opportunity to see different velocity serves with different spins. The drawback to practicing with another beginner is that neither of you are at the level to execute a variety of consistent serves. This is a drill that requires a skilled partner to deliver the serves.

Attacking The Net Drill

The final drill is an attacking net drill that requires a partner to feed the ball to the attacking partner. The feeding partner holds three balls and places the first deep to the forehand of the attacking partner. The attacking partner hits a deep forehand groundstroke return and begins to advance to the net. The feeding partner then places the second ball to the attacking partner's forehand, forcing a forehand approach shot deep to the baseline. The attacking partner continues to advance to the net, receives a ball to the forehand side from the feeder that is then volleyed by the attacking partner. (See Figures 11.18–11.22.)

Figure 11.18   Attacking player hits groundstroke.

Figure 11.19   Attacking player groundstroke follow through.

Figure 11.20   Attacking player returns approach shot.

Figure 11.21   Attacking player initiates move forward.

Figure 11.22   Attacking player moves forward and returns volley shot.

The sequence can be repeated to the backhand, mixed up with the attacking partner not knowing which direction the ball is being placed. Other shots including a second volley and overhead smash can be incorporated into the drill as skill improves. The attacking player can also work on placement with depth and at angles to gain the best advantage at the net. This is not a particularly easy drill, but you will be surprised how well you do because you do not have time to think and because the ball is being placed to you.

Practice is really important. The practice by yourself and partner practice drills will enable you to progress and increase your skill level more rapidly than simply listening to instruction and practicing only during that instructional time. Tennis is an easy game once you gain the skills to play it. Practice enables you to gain the skills in order to have fun.

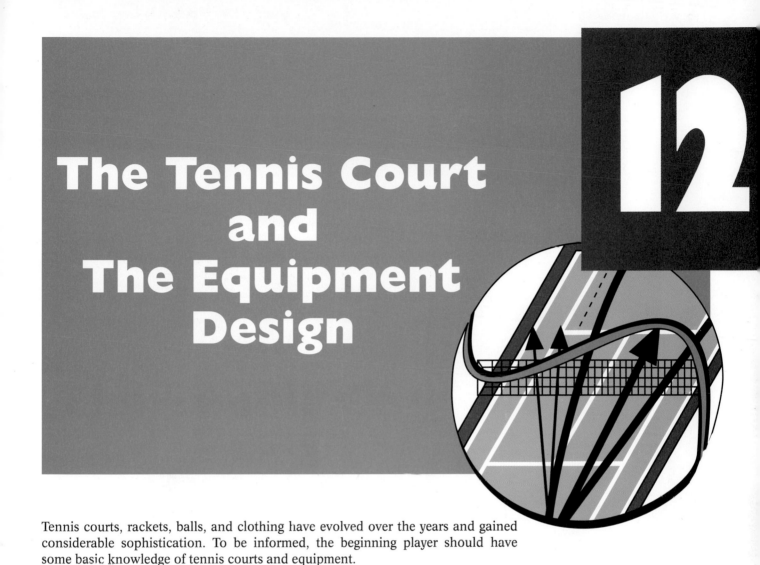

The Tennis Court and The Equipment Design

12

Tennis courts, rackets, balls, and clothing have evolved over the years and gained considerable sophistication. To be informed, the beginning player should have some basic knowledge of tennis courts and equipment.

THE TENNIS COURT

There are five categories of *tennis court surfaces*. *Grass courts* are traditional but have outlived their usefulness. Wimbledon is the only major professional tournament still played on a grass court. For normal play, the upkeep and expense involved in maintaining the surface is nearly prohibitive. There are few grass courts in the United States, and they are nearly extinct worldwide. Soft courts are popular throughout much of the world and east of the Mississippi River in the United States. The typical soft court is a *clay court*, and its surface provides a high bounce and a slow ball that encourage long baseline rallies. The term "clay court" is descriptive of the surface, composed of a claylike material and coarse sand. There are also a number of other "claylike" surfaces including shale and synthetic composites that play like clay. The clay surface poses a maintenance problem when reasonable play conditions are desired, because it requires watering and rolling.

The *all-weather* or *hard court* surfaces are extremely popular in the United States. This is the surface with which most developing players are familiar. The surface may be composed of asphalt or cement topping, which contributes to ease of maintenance and cleaning. Courts with this surface are usually public, and they are easily recognized because they provide a uniform, fast-bouncing action to the ball. The *synthetic surface*, is another type of hard surface that has been used by many players on their college campuses. The synthetic court surface is usually composed of a series of granulated rubber particles pulled together with an epoxy resin sprayed with a polyurethane coating and laid on a porous foundation. The court is designed to play like a naturally made court, but it is free of maintenance and cleaning problems. The synthetic court is called the Mercury Grassphalts Court, and it is one of several innovative courts. Another court surface is usually called a *carpet,* and it is used for indoor tournaments on the professional tennis tour. The carpet is laid over whatever existing surface is available, and that combination produces a fast court that encourages a serve-volley game.

A final interesting point with tennis court surfaces is that hard and synthetic courts are smoothed or roughened depending on the amount of play and rally circumstances expected in a certain geographical area. A high altitude location will tend to have a roughened surface to provide more opportunity for baseline play, while courts in low altitudes will have a smoother surface, since the density of the air allows for more rally situations.

Figure 12.1 Comparison of wood and composite wide-body rackets.

Figure 12.2 Assorted tennis rackets.

TENNIS RACKETS

Tennis rackets were at one time made of various woods, including ash or beech and combinations of perhaps sycamore, obeche, or mahogany. The wood racket was handcrafted, and the number of wood laminations indicated the quality of the racket. Wood rackets are now generally obsolete, replaced by modern technology's use of new materials (Figure 12.1). Composite rackets are designed with a combination of nylon, polyurethane, carbon, fiberglass, and graphite. Metal and aluminum rackets are still available, but as with wood rackets, they have been replaced by the composite racket. The most recent revolutionary racket development is the new wide-body racket that provides maximum power with greater control. They are stiffer rackets and they bend less at contact with the ball, providing more energy to the ball. There is more power in the wide-body, but the skill level of the player cannot always match the quality of the racket. As a result, emphasis in developing new technology includes ways of reducing the wide-body width, which in turn brings back more control (Figure 12.2).

Rackets have also changed in size over the last fifteen years ranging from a regular size, to a mid-size, to an oversize racket. The Prince racket was the first oversize racket, and now all companies are manufacturing oversize rackets. Shapes of racket heads range from pear-shaped to round and oblong.

Terms are used to describe the racket and what it is designed to accomplish. A *stiff* racket has less control and more power than flexible rackets. A *flexible* racket will provide more control but less power. The wide-body rackets were originally promoted with the concept that they would have power because they are stiff but also have a good degree of control that was usually characteristic of the flexible conventional oversize racket. The beginner needs a flexible racket with some stiffness to provide a little power or zip to the ball. As skill is developed, a decision on more stiffness or more flexibility becomes a personal choice.

Very stiff rackets have the potential of causing tennis elbow. Two other terms define stress on the elbow. *Shock* is a term that describes the contact of string to ball, producing a great amount of force. If a ball is hit off center there is a twisting action that produces considerable additional shock the closer the ball is to the frame at contact. A racket frame with considerable torque at contact will add to the potential for elbow distress. The second term, *vibration,* is defined as the lingering back and forth motion of the racket frame and strings after the ball has been hit. Other terms used by tennis players are *power, control, feel,* and *playability.* Each of these terms are also used in tennis publications that review racket strengths and weaknesses. Rackets are head light, balanced, and head heavy. They are light, semi-light, and medium in weight. The ideal area for contact with the ball is called a *sweetspot* (Figure 12.3), and it can be located below center, above center, elongated, and wide across center. Most sweet spots are located at center and above center, but they do vary. Sweetspots basically allow for a shot that is not hit quite on center to still rebound effectively. The larger the oversize racket, the larger the sweetspot, so the more chance for success. A stiffer racket stretches the sweetspot, and lowering of string tension increases a sweetspot's effectiveness. (S. Chirls, June, 1992, Sweet talk about the sweetspot, *Tennis,* p. 77). Racket grips are measured from 4⅛ inches to 4⅞ inches, with the widely used grips ranging from 4¼ to 4⅝ inches. Grips are composed of several types of material, with leather or new synthetic materials being the most useful and popular.

Prices of rackets range from an inexpensive, and probably worthless, 10 dollars to an exorbitant 300 or more dollars. It is a small wonder that consumers are confused. The beginning players should therefore use some kind of guide when purchasing a tennis racket.

The *guide to buying a racket* begins with price. It is acceptable to pay as much as one can afford, but the buyer should be reasonable. A good composite racket can be bought for between 60 and 75 dollars. The best racket is what feels good, so the player should try several before selecting one to purchase. Most tennis dealers and clubs will provide a "loaner" for practice for a charge of three to five dollars, then count that expense toward the purchase of a racket. Grip size should also be based to a great extent on how the grip feels, but a serve and volley player will want a larger grip than the baseline or all-purpose player. Most players buy a lightweight racket because it is easier to handle and places less stress on the elbow.

Rackets are purchased unstrung if they are of reasonable quality, and a decision has to be made regarding the type of string to use. There are two considerations to be made when *selecting string:* the type of string and the pounds at which the racket should be strung. There are basically two types of string: an expensive gut string (25 to 40 dollars), primarily for highly skilled tournament players, and a nylon base string that wears for a longer time, is less expensive, and is hardly discernible from the gut string for the average player. Nylon string ranges in cost from 10 to 35 dollars, and the selection is almost endless. There are oil hole strings, solid core strings, and composite strings that are all forms of nylon. Most nylon strings are acceptable, and a middle price seems to be a logical choice. The pounds at which the racket should be strung should follow the manufacturer's recommendation, and then as the player develops skill, the pound based on skill level and ability can be identified through a series of choices. String at the higher end of tension or pounds gives the player more control while lower tension or pounds enhance power. Thinner string (17 gauge is the thinnest) increases power and spin, while thicker strings (15 gauge) are more durable.

The beginning tennis player must understand that the expenses associated with being a player and the purchase of a racket continue to the purchase of a second, or backup racket, and to a restringing of a racket every month or two during the tennis season(s). When the racket seems to have lost the zip it once had or the strings begin to fray, it is time to have the racket restrung. *Restringing* can consist of a full restring job or a technique called running repairs. If there is still life in the racket, and the player is not at a tournament level of play, a stringer can replace a

Figure 12.3 Sweetspot.

Figure 12.4   Tennis stringer.

broken string. A beginning player can have running repairs done on the racket and save a little in cost. See Figure 12.4.

Tennis ball selection is another choice and expense to tennis play. A can of tennis balls ranges from two to four dollars and only lasts for two to three hours of play (if play is continuous and skillful). Discount stores and major sporting goods dealers often run specials for less than two dollars, but the player should be aware that there are many types of tennis balls for that price. For true bounce and longevity, balls should be a name-brand (Figure 12.5), and flaws or unknowns should be ignored. Pressurized balls don't last as long as hard core rubber tennis balls, but they are easier on elbows and they play with a true bounce. The hard core ball has a greater life expectancy but begins to bounce too high after extensive play. If a player lives at high altitude, the purchase of only high-altitude balls is required. There is a difference when playing at sea level and playing at 5,000 feet.

Figure 12.5   Tennis balls.

TENNIS CLOTHING

The selection of *tennis shorts or skirt and a tennis top* is totally up to the player. An investment of 10 dollars for a pair of shorts and a tee shirt to an investment in excess of 200 dollars for a designer pair of tennis shorts and top is the range for purchase of clothing (Figure 12.6).

Tennis shoes (Figure 12.7) and socks are a different matter expense-wise. The tennis shoe is designed for use on a tennis court and for the forward, backward, and lateral movement of the player. There are many stops and starts in tennis, and the toe of a tennis shoe is vulnerable to dragging and wearing out. Tennis shoes are sized as are dress shoes, and some tennis shoes also are measured by widths of wide or narrow. There are subtle considerations when selecting a tennis shoe. It must have a firm insole and a good arch support. It is very important that the back portion of the shoe that rests against the Achilles' tendon be soft and pliable, and that there be an absorbent heel cushion.

A check to determine how much abuse the toe of the shoe will take will help the player avoid a new purchase every three or four weeks. If the tennis shoe fits the player, if it provides good support, and if it won't wear out in a few weeks, it will probably cost 45 dollars or more, but it is what a player ought to buy. Socks, although not expensive, should also be purchased with quality in mind. A tennis sock should absorb perspiration, fit well, and be designed for tennis play.

Figure 12.6   Tennis clothing.

Figure 12.7   Tennis shoes.

Tournament Competition and Resources in Tennis

Part of developing as a beginning tennis player is to participate in tournaments to develop skills in a pressure situation. Another growth area is continuing to learn the game by being aware of professional tennis organizations, and by staying up-to-date by reading tennis publications and other materials that will provide new ideas. These are the resources in tennis.

HOW TO GET STARTED IN TENNIS COMPETITION

The United States has a wide assortment of *tennis tournaments*. Those that are of most interest to the beginning player are associated with recreation programs, college campus recreation programs, city tournaments, and club programs. There are tournaments for all types of players, from the novice beginner who is just now learning to hit a volley shot without ducking to a very skilled player. Tournaments usually are either ladder tournaments, single elimination or double elimination tournaments, inter-club, or a social round robin mixed doubles tournament. All are fun to play in with the correct perspective. Some are more competitive than others, and the player has to understand which are the more competitive and which are designed as a social function.

Ladder tournaments are found in all situations, including most campus recreation programs. They allow players to play at their own level by challenging individuals of similar skill, but positioned higher on the ladder based on earlier success demonstrated through winning. Club competition is a highly competitive league-type play in which records are kept and league standings are established. There are rewards for a team finishing first and second in a league, with a team or teams advancing to another round of competitive play. All programs have single and double elimination tournaments with ratings, including novice, C, B, A, and open divisions. Some are sanctioned by the *United States Tennis Association* (USTA) and require membership in that organization in order to participate. Some tournaments are identified by a rating scale, usually through the USTA National Rating Tennis Program. There are also age division tournaments that have an open competition under 35 years of age, then an age division, including 35 and over, 40 and over, 45 and over, 55 and over, 65 and over, etc. Most single or double elimination tournaments are played through a period of a week and a player may play 5 or 6 matches if the play continues all the way to the championship. The number of matches depends on the size of a draw for the tournament (a draw is the number of entrants).

The *USTA National Rating Program* has become a popular device for rating players, not only for tournament play, but for social play to help people identify their level of skill so that a match can be an equal competition. The rating scale is established from 1.0 through 7.0. The lower the rating classification, the closer to a beginner, and the higher the rating, the closer to a professional player. The classification of 3.0 to 5.0 seems to be the typical club player rating and is probably a major first goal for a developing player. The beginner usually starts at the 1.0 through the 2.5 level and progresses rapidly through the early classifications. The rating program provides a descriptive version of each classification, and many tennis teachers are now able to use the rating objectively and systematically. In order for you to be able to rate yourself, Table 13.1 gives you a view of the National Tennis Rating Program categories.

TEN

TENNIS RESOURCES

There are numerous textbooks and periodicals that help you to learn to play tennis and to continue to develop skills and knowledge associated with the game. There are also tennis associations designed to promote the game in community and tennis club environments.

The USTA is the most well known agency or organization designed to promote tennis at every level of play and competition. To play in sanctioned USTA tournaments, membership in the USTA is required. The same group sponsors the National Tennis Rating Program. But, perhaps most important, the USTA supplies educational groups with an assortment of tennis publications and films. One publication circulated to members of the USTA is entitled *Tennis,* along with a second magazine supplement called *Tennis USTA* which is also sold at newsstands. Other publications by the USTA include general textbooks, material for group instruction and for teaching tennis, strategy material, program planning, tennis information, and rules-regulations. A membership with the USTA is a small investment for the beginning player, because membership is inexpensive. The benefits for a serious player are excellent, and the organization really does function for the promotion of tennis. The USTA membership address is: USTA/Membership Department/ 70 West Red Oak Lane/ White Plains, NY 90604.

There are also tennis organizations affiliated with the USTA. These are described as *sectional offices and state organizations.* Both of these groups sponsor tennis tournaments and also have the major role of promoting tennis. With a USTA membership, the member also receives newsletters from

TABLE 13.1 ● NTRP Rating Categories

1.0 This player is just starting to play tennis.

1.5 This player has limited experience and is still working primarily on getting the ball into play.

2.0 This player needs on-court experience. This player has obvious stroke weaknesses but is familiar with basic positions for singles and doubles play.

2.5 This player is learning to judge where the ball is going although court coverage is weak. This player can sustain a rally of slow pace with other players of the same ability.

3.0 This player is consistent when hitting medium paced shots, but is not comfortable with all strokes and lacks control when trying for directional intent, depth, or power.

3.5 This player has achieved improved stroke dependability and direction on moderate shots, but still lacks depth and variety. This player is starting to exhibit more aggressive net play, has improved court coverage, and is developing teamwork in doubles.

4.0 This player has dependable strokes, including directional intent and depth on both forehand and backhand sides on moderate shots, plus the ability to use lobs, overheads, approach shots and volleys with some success. This player occasionally forces errors when serving and teamwork in doubles is evident.

4.5 This player has begun to master the use of power and spins and is beginning to handle pace, has sound footwork, can control depth of shots, and is beginning to vary tactics according to opponents. This player can hit first serves with power and accuracy and place the second serve and is able to rush net successfully.

5.0 This player has good shot anticipation and frequently has an outstanding shot or exceptional consistency around which a game may be structured. This player can regularly hit winners or force errors off of short balls and can put away volleys, can successfully execute lobs, drop shots, half volleys and overhead smashes and has good depth and spin on most second serves.

5.5 This player has developed power and/or consistency as a major weapon. This player can vary strategies and styles of play in a competitive situation and hits dependable shots in a stress situation.

6.0 to 7.0 These players will generally not need NTRP ratings. Rankings or past rankings will speak for themselves. The 6.0 player typically has had intensive training for national tournament competition at the junior level and collegiate levels and has obtained a sectional and/or national ranking. The 6.5 player has a reasonable chance of succeeding at the 7.0 level and has extensive satellite tournament experience. The 7.0 is a world class player who is committed to tournament competition on the international level and whose major source of income is tournament prize winnings.

Once you have determined your rating, write the appropriate rating number on your USTA membership card under "NTRP". In order to participate in USTA league or NTRP tournaments, you must get verified by a sectionally approved NTRP verifier. Your NTRP rating will help you find challenging opponents no matter where you play.   (Printed with permission of the USTA)

sectional and state organizations. The local state and sectional organizations also rate players and carry on the work of the USTA at the local level.

Tennis publications, both trade magazines and books, and textbooks, are plentiful. Besides *Tennis* and *Tennis USTA* there are such magazines as *Racquet,* an avant garde publication, and *International Tennis Players* that covers the professional circuit. Of the numerous books on the market there are several that should be mentioned because they serve as resource information and are worthwhile supplements to this text. They include:

● Vic Braden and Bill Bruns, *Tennis for the Future.* Vic Braden is known for his ability to keep tennis simple and to accurately biomechanically analyze the strokes of the game. This book reflects that ability.

- James E. Bryant, *Tennis: A Guide for the Developing Tennis Player*. A college textbook that is designed to take the player from a beginner's level and progress through development stages to a lifetime of enjoyable tennis experience.

- Paul Douglas, *Tennis for the Future*. Douglas covers the game of tennis in depth with extensive information and graphic presentation of the strokes and overall view of the game.

- Dick Gould, *Tennis Anyone?* This is a college text written by the leading collegiate tennis coach in the country. The book is for beginners and provides helpful information for beginning play.

- Clancy Moore and M. B. Chafin, *Tennis Everyone*. This is a basic collegiate text for beginning tennis players that provides a base for understanding and application of the game.

In addition to magazines and books, there are other resources to either enhance your tennis skills or your tennis background. There are a number of films and videos on tennis. The videos are particularly helpful since they tend to be up-to-date and innovative in presenting "how-to-play" concepts. These videos include skill instruction, sybervision, highlights of great matches, and tennis tips. Vic Braden has produced some quality videotapes. Of these, two that meet a beginner's needs are *Maximizing Your Tennis Potential* and *How to Play—Strokes and Strategies*. Dr. Jim Loehr, mentioned earlier in Chapter 7, has produced a mental-aspects-of-tennis video entitled *Mental Toughness Training — The 16 Second Cure*.

There are also several cable networks including ESPN and Sportschannel that produce programs that contain a weekly series of tennis tips and instruction for the interested tennis viewer. These videos and television programs are probably the most helpful because they are current and feature leading authorities on tennis.

Television also provides extensive coverage of major tennis events including The Australian Open, French Open, US Open, and Wimbledon. In addition, smaller tournaments constantly surface on television along with an occasional collegiate tennis competition. These are also instructional in the sense that if you watch skilled players you can pick up new techniques, skills and a feeling for the game. Finally, there is even an International Tennis Hall of Fame located in Newport, Rhode Island, that publishes a newsletter four times per year. If you become really hooked on tennis and want to gain a historical or traditional view of the game, the Tennis Hall of Fame simply adds to your enjoyment.

A final, but very important resource for a player who continues to develop following group instruction at the college/university level is a *teaching professional*. As an occasional review, or to have technique analyzed, a teaching professional is of value. There are several points to remember concerning a teaching professional, or for that matter, an instructor at the college level who teaches tennis. That professional should know mechanics of stroke execution, should know how to present the information in an interesting and informative way, and should be able to analyze stroke mistakes. Go to a teaching professional for lessons, then go back and play for an extended period. It doesn't make any difference what kind of stroke development occurs in lessons if that stroke can't be assimilated in tennis match conditions.

Resources are important for a beginning tennis player. The selection of the proper resources is important, and must be done with some degree of insight. A player needs to keep up with changes in tennis, and needs to have enough knowledge to discuss tennis intelligently.

Glossary of Terms

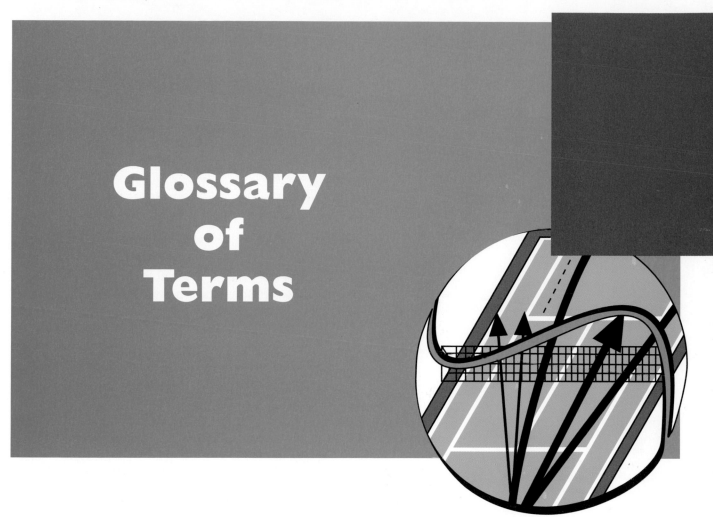

Ad: In a tie game, ad represents advantage of one point to the server or receiver.

Ad court: The left service court.

Ad in: Advantage to the server.

Ad out: Advantage to the receiver.

Aerial game: The use of overhead smashes and defensive and offensive lobs as part of the total tennis game.

American twist service: Serve that has a reverse side spin applied to the ball.

Anxiety: State of mental pressure that causes a reduction in physical performance.

Approach shot: A groundstroke hit inside the baseline toward the net.

Australian doubles formation: A two-player alignment in doubles that places the net player in a position perpendicular from server to the net.

Backhand: Balls hit on the non-racket side of the body.

Ballistic warm-up: Physically moving the body to prepare for a match.

Baseline: The end of the court located 39 feet from the net.

Center mark: The division line on the baseline that separates the right side from the left side.

Center strap: The strap that anchors the middle of the net to the court at a 3-foot height.

Chop: An exaggerated slice stroke.

Closed face: Position of the racket face as it is turned down toward the court.

Complex overhead smash: Includes a scissors kick in addition to the orthodox overhead smash as the player jumps to hit the ball.

Control: The measure of how effectively the racket permits the player to place the ball on various shots.

Conventional doubles: Two players in a doubles match who are positioned as one up (at net), one back (at baseline).

Close in: Move in on the net following an approach shot, an overhead smash, or a volley.

Cross court: Hitting the ball at an angle across the width of the court with the net as the central boundary.

Defensive lob: A ball hit to give the defending player a chance to recover from an opponent's offensive shot.

Deuce: A tie score in games at 40-40 or beyond.

Dink shot: A sidespin drop shot hit at an angle from the net to the other side of the court.

Division of play: The division of the court between the opponent's position and the other player's position that provides an equal distance to reach a forehand or backhand shot.

Double fault: The serving of two illegal serves during one service point.

Down the line: A shot hit down a sideline in a direct line from the player.

Drive: A ball hit with force.

Drop shot: A ball hit from a groundstoke position that barely clears the net and dies on the opponent's side of the court.

Drop volley: Same shot as drop shot, but from a position of hitting the ball before it bounces on the court.

Dump shot: A push action that guides the ball to an open area beyond the opponent's side of the court.

Etiquette: Rules of behavior on a tennis court.

Feel: The general kinesthetic sense of how a racket feels in the hand of the player.

Fault: An illegally hit serve.

Flat serve: A serve hit with little spin and with a basically flat trajectory.

Flexible racket: A description of a racket that has more control and less power.

Forecourt: Part of the tennis court between the net and the service court line.

Forehand: Balls hit on the racket side of the body.

Groundstroke: The act of hitting a ball following the bounce of the ball on the court.

Half volley: A ball hit immediately following the bounce on the court.

Homebase: A term to describe the position a player assumes who prefers to play from the baseline and rally.

Let: A point played over due to interference or a serve replayed due to an otherwise legal serve touching the net.

Lob: A ball hit up over the net player, driving that player back away from the net.

Love: A zero score.

Match: The best two of three sets in most play situations.

Moonball: A lofted topspin shot that is designed to change the pace of a rally. Halfway between a lob and a groundstroke.

Net play: Generally, offensive play near the net with volley shots and approach shots characteristic of the shots hit.

Non-racket shoulder: The shoulder of the arm on which the racket is not grasped (e.g., right-hand player's non-racket shoulder is the left shoulder).

Non-racket side of the body: The same description as for non-racket shoulder, but refers to the whole side of the body (e.g., right-handed player's left side of the body).

Offensive lob: A lofted shot hit deep to the opponent's baseline with topspin ball action used to chase the opponent away from the net.

Open face: Position of the racket face as it is turned up to the sky.

Orthodox overhead smash: An overhead smash that requires no foot position exchange.

Overhead smash: An offensive throwing action stroke similar to a serve in motion, but delivered at the net back to the baseline.

Pace: A ball hit with the same consistency, usually with some degree of velocity.

Percentage tennis: A philosophical strategy that is based on forcing the opponent to make the error rather than you hitting all winning shots.

Playability: A subjective measure of how the racket responds in general during play.

Power: Also described as a "sweetspot," the measure of the "power zone" of the racket.

Punching action: Hitting the ball with little backswing or follow through.

Racket face: The strings of the racket as they face the oncoming ball during a stroke sequence.

Racket head: The total racket area that includes the string and the material around the face.

Racket shoulder: The shoulder of the arm with which the player grasps the racket.

Racket side of the body: Same description as for the racket shoulder but includes the whole side of the body.

Rally: A sustained play of a point, usually associated with hitting only groundstrokes from the baseline area. It never refers to hitting a ball on the fly as in a volley.

Return of serve: The act of hitting a ball back off a serve.

Service court line: The line that is the base of the service courts and that is parallel to the net and baseline.

Set: Represents the winning of six games with a margin of 2 games, or winning by a score of 7-5 or 7-6.

Sidespin: Spin action imparted on a ball so that the ball will land on the court and kick away from the person hitting the ball. Ball is hit on the backside portion to give the sidespin effect.

Slice serve: A serve hit with side spin.

Social doubles: Tennis played in a friendly atmosphere with a player alignment usually of one up-one back.

Stability: The ability of a racket to resist the twisting motion when the ball is hit off center.

Stiff racket: A description of a racket that has less control and more power.

Strategy: The planning of an attack when competing against another player or a doubles team.

Stretch warm-up: A static stretching of muscle groups to prepare for a match.

Sweetspot: The surface area of the racket face that provides a functional rebound area as the ball strikes the racket at contact.

Swinging action: A groundstroke movement that represents the motor pattern of swinging as in a baseball bat swing.

Throwing action: A serving or overhead smash motion that represents a throwing pattern as in throwing a baseball.

Timing: The coordinated effort of hitting a ball at the right synchronized point.

Topspin: A ball hit with an overspin rotation action.

Topspin serve: A serve that has a forward or overspin rotation applied to the ball. The end result is a high-bouncing, quick rebound from the tennis court.

Underspin: A ball hit with backspin rotation. The ball will have a tendency to float and slow down when striking the tennis court.

Vibration: The measure of how well a racket absorbs vibration at contact with the ball.

Warming up: The act of physically preparing for a tennis match.

Warming down: The act of cooling off the body in a sequential logical order to complete the finish of a tennis match.

Waste land: The area between the baseline and the service court line that a player should never set up in to begin a rally.

USTA Tennis Rules

Explanatory Note

The following Rules and Cases and Decisions are the official Code of the International Tennis Federation, of which the United States Tennis Association is a member. USTA Comments have the same weight and force in USTA tournaments as do ITF Cases and Decisions.

When a match is played without officials the principles and guidelines set forth in the USTA Publication, The Code, shall apply in any situation not covered by the rules.

Except where otherwise stated every reference in these Rules to the masculine includes the feminine gender.

The Singles Game

RULE 1

The Court

The court shall be a rectangle 78 feet (23.77m.) long and 27 feet (8.23m.) wide.

> **USTA Comment:** *See Rule 34 for a doubles court.*

It shall be divided across the middle by a net suspended from a cord or metal cable of a maximum diameter of one-third of an inch (0.8cm.), the ends of which shall be attached to, or pass over, the tops of two posts, which shall be not more than 6 inches (15cm.) square or 6 inches (15cm.) in diameter. These posts shall not be higher than 1 inch (2.5cm.) above the top of the net cord. The centres of the posts shall be 3 feet (0.914m.) outside the court on each side and the height of the posts shall be such that the top of the cord or metal cable shall be 3 feet 6 inches (1.07m.) above the ground.

When a combined doubles (see Rule 34) and singles court with a doubles net is used for singles, the net must be supported to a height of 3 feet 6 inches (1.07m.) by means of two posts, called "singles sticks", which shall be not more than 3 inches (7.5cm.) square or 3 inches (7.5cm.) in diameter. The centres of the singles sticks shall be 3 feet (0.914m.) outside the singles court on each side.

The net shall be extended fully so that it fills completely the space between the two posts and shall be of sufficiently small mesh to prevent the ball passing through. The height of the net shall be 3 feet (0.914m.) at the centre, where it shall be held down taut by a strap not more than 2 inches (5cm.) wide and completely white in colour. There shall be a band covering the cord or metal cable and the top of the net of not less than 2 inches (5cm.) nor more than 2½ inches (6.3cm.) in depth on each side and completely white in colour.

> **USTA Comment:** *An approved method for obtaining proper net tautness is: Loosen the center strap. Tighten the net cord until it is approximately 40 inches above the ground, being careful not to overtighten the net. Tighten the center strap until the center of the net is 36 inches above the ground. These measurements should always be made before the first match of the day.*

There shall be no advertisement on the net, strap, band or singles sticks.

The lines bounding the ends and sides of the Court shall respectively be called the base-lines and the side-lines. On each side of the net, at a distance of 21 feet (6.40m.) from it and parallel with it, shall be drawn the service-lines. The space on each side of the net between the service-line and the side-lines shall be divided into two equal parts called the service-courts by the centre service-line, which must be 2 inches (5cm.) in width, drawn half-way between, and parallel with, the side-lines. Each base-line shall be bisected by an imaginary continuation of the centre service-line to a line 4 inches (10cm.) in length and 2 inches (5cm.) in width called the centre mark drawn inside the Court, at right angles to and in contact with such base-lines. All other lines shall be not less than 1 inch (2.5 cm) nor more than 2 inches (5cm.) in width, except the base-line, which may be not more than 4 inches (10cm.) in width, and all measurements shall be made to the outside of the lines. All lines shall be of uniform colour.

If advertising or any other material is placed at the back of the court, it may not contain white, or yellow. A light colour may only be used if this does not interfere with the vision of the players.

If advertisements are placed on the chairs of the Linesmen sitting at the back of the court, they may not contain white, or yellow. A light colour may only be used if this does not interfere with the vision of the players.

ITF Note: In the case of the *Davis Cup* or other Official Championships of the International Tennis Federation, there shall be a space behind each base-line of not less than 21 feet (6.4m.), and at the sides of not less than 12 feet (3.66m.). The chairs of the linesmen may be placed at the back of the court within the 21 feet or at the side of the court within the 12 feet, provided they do not protrude into that area more than 3 feet (.914m).

RULE 2

Permanent Fixtures

The permanent fixtures of the Court shall include not only the net, posts, singles sticks, cord or metal cable, strap and band, but also, where there are any such, the back and side stops, the stands, fixed or movable seats and chairs round the Court, and their occupants, all other fixtures around and above the Court, and the Umpire, Net-cord Judge, Foot-fault Judge, Linesmen and Ball Boys when in their respective places.

ITF Note: For the purpose of this Rule, the word "Umpire" comprehends the Umpire, the persons entitled to a seat on the Court, and all those persons designated to assist the Umpire in the conduct of a match.

RULE 3

The Ball

The ball shall have a uniform outer surface and shall be white or yellow in colour. If there are any seams, they shall be stitchless.

The ball shall be more than two and a half inches (6.35cm.) and less than two and five-eighths inches (6.67cm.) in diameter, and more than two ounces (56.7 grams) and less than two and one-sixteenth ounces (58.5 grams) in weight.

The ball shall have a bound of more than 53 inches (135cm.) and less than 58 inches (147cm.) when dropped 100 inches (254cm.) upon a concrete base.

The ball shall have a forward deformation of more than .220 of an inch (56cm) and less than .290 of an inch (.74cm) and a return deformation of more than .350 of an inch (89cm.) and less than .425 of an inch (1.08cm) at 18 lb (8.165kg) load. The two deformation figures shall be the averages of three individual readings along three axes of the ball and no two individual readings shall differ by more than .030 of an inch (.08cm.) in each case.

For play above 4,000 feet (1219m) in altitude above sea level, two additional types of ball may be used. The first type is identical to those described above except that the bound shall be more than 48 inches (121.92cm) and less than 53 inches (135cm) and the ball shall have an internal pressure that is greater than the external pressure. This type of tennis ball is commonly known as a pressurized ball. The second type is identical to those described above except that they shall have a bound of more than 53 inches (135cm) and less than 58 inches (147cm) and shall have an internal

pressure that is approximately equal to the external pressure and have been acclimatized for 60 days or more at the altitude of the specific tournament. This type of tennis ball is commonly known as a zero-pressure or non-pressurized ball.

All tests for bound, size and deformation shall be made in accordance with the Regulations in the Appendix hereto.

RULE 4

The Racket

Rackets failing to comply with the following specifications are not approved for play under the Rules of Tennis:

(a) The hitting surface of the racket shall be flat and consist of a pattern of crossed strings connected to a frame and alternately interlaced or bonded where they cross; and the stringing pattern shall be generally uniform, and in particular not less dense in the centre than in any other area. The strings shall be free of attached objects and protrusions other than those utilized solely and specifically to limit or prevent wear and tear or vibration and which are reasonable in size and placement for such purposes.

(b) The frame of the racket shall not exceed 32 inches (81 28cm.) in overall length, including the handle and 12½ inches (31.75cm.) in overall width The strung surface shall not exceed 15½ inches (39.37cm.) in overall length, and 11½ inches (29.21cm.) in overall width.

(c) The frame, including the handle, shall be free of attached objects and devices other than those utilized solely and specifically to limit or prevent wear and tear or vibration, or to distribute weight. Any objects and devices must be reasonable in size and placement for such purposes.

(d) The frame, including the handle and the strings, shall be free of any device which makes it possible to change materially the shape of the racket, or to change the weight distribution, during the playing of a point.

The International Tennis Federation shall rule on the question of whether any racket or prototype complies with the above specifications or is otherwise approved, or not approved, for play. Such ruling may be undertaken on its own initiative, or upon application by any party with a bona fide interest therein, including any player, equipment manufacturer or National Association or members thereof. Such rulings and applications shall be made in accordance with the applicable Review and Hearing Procedures of the International Tennis Federation, copies of which may be obtained from the office of the Secretary.

Case 1. Can there be more than one set of strings on the hitting surface of a racket?

Decision. No. The rule clearly mentions a pattern, and not patterns, of crossed strings.

Case 2. Is the stringing pattern of a racket considered to be generally uniform and flat if the strings are on more than one plane?

Decision. No.

Case 3. Can a vibration dampening device be placed on the strings of a racket and if so, where can it be placed?

Decision. Yes; but such devices may only be placed outside the pattern of crossed strings.

Case 4. In the course of play a player accidentally breaks the strings of his racket. Can he continue to play with the racket in this condition?

Decision. Yes.

RULE 5

Server and Receiver

The players shall stand on opposite sides of the net; the player who first delivers the ball shall be called the Server, and the other the Receiver.

Case 1. Does a player, attempting a stroke, lose the point if he crosses an imaginary line in the extension of the net,

(a) before striking the ball,

(b) after striking the ball?

Decision. He does not lose the point in either case by crossing the imaginary line and provided he does not enter the lines bounding his opponent's Court (Rule 20 (e)). In regard to hindrance, his opponent may ask for the decision of the Umpire under Rules 21 and 25.

Case 2. The Server claims that the Receiver must stand within the lines bounding his Court. Is this necessary?

Decision. No. The Receiver may stand wherever he pleases on his own side of the net.

RULE 6

Choice of Ends and Service

The choice of ends and the right to be Server or Receiver in the first game shall be decided by toss. The player winning the toss may choose or require his opponent to choose:

(a) The right to be Server or Receiver, in which case the other player shall choose the end; or

(b) The end, in which case the other player shall choose the right to be Server or Receiver.

Case 1. Do players have the right to new choices if the match is postponed or suspended before it has started?

Decision. Yes. The toss stands, but new choices may be made with respect to service and end.

> **USTA Comment:** *The toss shall be made before the warm-up. Choices should be made promptly after the toss and are irrevocable, except when the match is postponed or suspended before the start of the match.*

RULE 7

The Service

The service shall be delivered in the following manner. Immediately before commencing to serve, the Server shall stand with both feet at rest behind (i.e. further from the net than) the base-line, and within the imaginary continuations of the centre-mark and sideline. The Server shall then project the ball by hand into the air in any direction and before it hits the ground strike it with his racket, and the delivery shall be deemed to have been completed at the moment of the impact of the racket and the ball. A player with the use of only one arm may utilize his racket for the projection.

> **USTA Comment:** *The service begins when the Server takes a ready position (i.e. both feet at rest behind the baseline) and ends when his racket makes contact with the ball, or when he misses the ball in attempting to serve it.*

> **USTA Comment:** *There is no restriction regarding the kind of service which may be used; that is, the player may use an underhand or overhand service at his discretion.*

Case 1. May the Server in a singles game take his stand behind the portion of the base-line between the side-lines of the Singles Court and the Doubles Court?

Decision. No.

> **USTA Comment:** *The server may stand anywhere in back of the baseline between the imaginary extensions of the center mark and the singles sideline.*

Case 2. If a player, when serving, throws up two or more balls instead of one, does he lose that service?

Decision. No. A let should be called, but if the Umpire regards the action as deliberate he may take action under Rule 21.

RULE 8

Foot Fault

(a) The Server shall throughout the delivery of the service:

(i) Not change his position by walking or running. The Server shall not by slight movements of the feet which do not materially affect the location originally taken up by him, be deemed "to change his position by walking or running."

(ii) Not touch, with either foot, any area other than that behind the base-line within the imaginary extensions of the centre mark and side-lines.

(b) The word "foot" means the extremity of the leg below the ankle.

> **USTA Comment:** *This rule covers the most decisive stroke in the game, and there is no justification for its not being obeyed by players and enforced by officials. No official has the right to instruct any umpire to disregard violations of it. In a non-officiated match, the Receiver, or his partner, may call foot faults after all efforts (appeal to the server, request for an umpire, etc.) have failed and the foot faulting is so flagrant as to be clearly perceptible from the Receiver's side.*
>
> *It is improper for any official to warn a player that he is in danger of having a foot fault called on him. On the other hand, if a player asks for an explanation of how he foot faulted, either the Line Umpire or the Chair Umpire should give him that information.*

RULE 9

Delivery of Service

(a) In delivering the service, the Server shall stand alternately behind the right and left Courts beginning from the right in every game. If service from a wrong half of the Court occurs and is undetected, all play resulting from such wrong service or services shall stand, but the inaccuracy of station shall be corrected immediately it is discovered.

(b) The ball served shall pass over the net and hit the ground within the Service Court which is diagonally opposite, or upon any line bounding such Court, before the Receiver returns it.

RULE 10

Service Fault

The Service is a fault:

(a) If the Server commits any breach of Rules 7, 8 or 9(b);

(b) If he misses the ball in attempting to strike it;

(c) If the ball served touches a permanent fixture (other than the net, strap or band) before it hits the ground.

Case 1. After throwing a ball up preparatory to serving, the Server decides not to strike at it and catches it instead. Is it a fault?

Decision. No.

> **USTA Comment:** *As long as the Server makes no attempt to strike the ball, it is immaterial whether he catches it in his hand or on his racket or lets it drop to the ground.*

Case 2. In serving in a singles game played on a Doubles Court with doubles posts and singles sticks, the ball hits a singles stick and then hits the ground within the lines of the correct Service Court. Is this a fault or a let?

Decision. In serving it is a fault, because the singles stick, the doubles post, and that portion of the net, or band between them are permanent fixtures. (Rules 2 and 10, and note to Rule 24.).

> **USTA Comment:** *The significant point governing Case 2 is that the part of the net and band "outside" the singles sticks is not part of the net over which this singles match is being played. Thus such a serve is a fault under the provisions of Article (c) above . . . By the same token, this would be a fault also if it were a singles game played with permanent posts in the singles position. See Case 1 under Rule 24 for difference between "service" and "good return" with respect to a ball hitting a net post.*

RULE 11

Second Service

After a fault (if it is the first fault) the Server shall serve again from behind the same half of the Court from which he served that fault, unless the service was from the wrong half, when, in accordance with Rule 9, the Server shall be entitled to one service only from behind the other half.

Case 1. A player serves from a wrong Court. He loses the point and then claims it was a fault because of his wrong station.

Decision. The point stands as played and the next service should be from the correct station according to the score.

Case 2. The point score being 15 all, the Server, by mistake, serves from the left-hand Court. He wins the point. He then serves again from the right-hand Court, delivering a fault. This mistake in station is then discovered. Is he entitled to the previous point? From which Court should he next serve?

Decision. The previous point stands. The next service should be from the left-hand Court, the score being 30/15, and the Server has served one fault.

RULE 12

When To Serve

The Server shall not serve until the Receiver is ready. If the latter attempts to return the service, he shall be deemed ready. If, however, the Receiver signifies that he is not ready, he may not claim a fault because the ball does not hit the ground within the limits fixed for the service.

> **USTA Comment:** *The Server must Wait until the Receiver is ready for the second service as well as the first, and if the Receiver claims to be not ready and does not make any effort to return a service, the Server's claim for the point may not be honored even though the service was good. However, the Receiver, having indicated he is ready, may not become unready unless some outside interference takes place.*

RULE 13

The Let

In all cases where a let has to be called under the rules, or to provide for an interruption to play, it shall have the following interpretations:

(a) When called solely in r•espect of a service that one service only shall be replayed.

(b) When called under any other circumstance, the point shall be replayed.

Case 1. A service is interrupted by some cause outside those defined in Rule 14. Should the service only be replayed?

Decision. No, the whole point must be replayed.

> **USTA Comment:** *Case 1 refers to a second serve, and the decision means that if the interruption occurs during delivery of the second service, the Server gets two serves. Example: On a second service a linesman calls "fault" and immediately corrects it, the Receiver meanwhile having let the ball go by. The Server is entitled to two serves, on this ground: The corrected call means that the Server has put the ball into play with a good service, and once the ball is in play and a let is called, the point must be replayed. Note, however, that if the serve is an unmistakable ace—that is, the Umpire is sure the erroneous call had no part in the Receiver's inability to play the ball—the point should be decided for the Server.*
>
> *If a delay between first and second serves is caused by the Receiver, by an official or by an outside interference the whole point shall be replayed; if the delay is caused by the Server, the Server has one serve to come. A spectator's outcry (of "out", "fault" or other) is not a valid basis for replay of a point, but action should be taken to prevent a recurrence.*

Case 2. If a ball in play becomes broken, should a let be called?
Decision. Yes.

> **USTA Comment:** *A ball shall be regarded as having become "broken" if, in the opinion of the Umpire, it is found to have lost compression to the point of being unfit for further play, or unfit for any reason, and it is clear the defective ball was the one in play.*

RULE 14

The "Let" in Service

The service is a let:

(a) If the ball served touches the net, strap or band, and is otherwise good, or, after touching the net, strap or band, touches the Receiver or anything which he wears or carries before hitting the ground.

(b) If a service or a fault is delivered when the Receiver is not ready (see Rule 12).

In case of a let, that particular service shall not count, and the Server shall serve again, but a service let does not annul a previous fault

RULE 15

Order of Service

At the end of the first game the Receiver shall become Server, and the Server Receiver; and so on alternately in all the subsequent games of a match. If a player serves out of turn, the player who ought to have served shall serve as soon as the mistake is discovered, but all points scored before such discovery shall be reckoned. If a game shall have been completed before such discovery, the order of service remains as altered. A fault served before such discovery shall not be reckoned.

RULE 16

When Players Change Ends

The players shall change ends at the end of the first, third and every subsequent alternate game of each set, and at the end of each set unless the total number of games in such set is even, in which case the change is not made until the end of the first game of the next set.

If a mistake is made and the correct sequence is not followed the players must take up their correct station as soon as the discovery is made and follow their original sequence.

RULE 17

The Ball in Play

A ball is in play from the moment at which it is delivered in service. Unless a fault or a let is called it remains in play until the point is decided.

> **USTA Comment:** *A point is not decided simply when, or because, a good shot has clearly passed a player, or when an apparently bad shot passes over a baseline or sideline. An outgoing ball is still definitely in play until it actually strikes the ground, backstop or a permanent fixture (other than the net, posts, singles sticks, cord or metal cable, strap or band), or a player. The same applies to a good ball, bounding after it has landed in the proper court. A ball that becomes imbedded in the net is out of play.*
>
> **USTA Comment:** *When a ball is hit into the net and the player on the other side, thinking the ball Is coming over, strikes at it and hits the net he loses the point if his touching the net occurs while the ball is still in play.*

Case 1. A player fails to make a good return. No call is made and the ball remains in play. May his opponent later claim the point after the rally has ended?

Decision. No. The point may not be claimed if the players continue to play after the error has been made, provided the opponent was not hindered.

> **USTA Comment:** *An out call on A's shot to B's court must be made before B's return has either gone out of play or been hit by A. See Case 3 under Rule 29 regarding this situation in an umpired match.*

RULE 18

Server Wins Point

The Server wins the point:

(a) If the ball served, not being a let under Rule 14, touches the Receiver or anything which he wears or carries, before it hits the ground:

(b) If the Receiver otherwise loses the point as provided by Rule 20.

RULE 19

Receiver Wins Point

The Receiver wins the point:

(a) If the Server serves two consecutive faults;

(b) If the Server otherwise loses the point as provided by Rule 20.

RULE 20

Player Loses Point

A player loses the point if:

(a) He fails, before the ball in play has hit the ground twice consecutively, to return it directly over the net (except as provided in Rule 24(a) or (c)); or

(b) He returns the ball in play so that it hits the ground, a permanent fixture, or other object, outside any of the lines which bound his opponent's Court (except as provided in Rule 24(a) or (c)); or

> **USTA Comment:** *A ball hitting a scoring device or other object attached to a net post results in loss of point to the striker.*

(c) He volleys the ball and fails to make a good return even when standing outside the Court; or

(d) In playing the ball he deliberately carries or catches it on his racket or deliberately touches it with his racket more than once; or

> **USTA Comment:** *Only when there is a definite "second push" by the player does his shot become illegal, with consequent loss of point. The word 'deliberately' is the key word in this rule. Two hits occurring in the course of a single continuous swing are not deemed a double hit.*

(e) He or his racket (in his hand or otherwise) or anything which he wears or carries touches the net, posts, singles sticks, cord or metal cable, strap or band, or the ground within his opponent's Court at any time while the ball is in play; or

> **USTA Comment:** *Touching a pipe support that runs across the court at the bottom of the net is interpreted as touching the net. See USTA Comment under Rule 23 for a ball which hits a pipe support.*

(f) He volleys the ball before it has passed the net; or

(g) The ball in play touches him or anything that he wears or carries, except his racket in his hand or hands; or

> **USTA Comment:** *This loss of point occurs regardless of whether the player is inside or outside the bounds of his court when the ball touches him.*

(h) He throws his racket at and hits the ball; or

(i) He deliberately and materially changes the shape of his racket during the playing of the point.

Case 1. In serving, the racket flies from the Server's hand and touches the net before the ball has touched the ground. Is this a fault, or does the player lose the point?

Decision. The Server loses the point because his racket touches the net whilst the ball is in play (Rule 20 *(e)*).

Case 2. In serving, the racket flies from the Server's hand and touches the net after the ball has touched the ground outside the proper court. Is this a fault, or does the player lose the point?

Decision. This is a fault because the ball was out of play when the racket touched the net.

Case 3. A and B are playing against C and D, A is serving to D, C touches the net before the ball touches the ground. A fault is then called because the service falls outside the Service Court. Do C and D lose the point?

Decision. The call "fault" is an erroneous one. C and D had already lost the point before "fault" could be called, because C touched the net whilst the ball was in play (Rule 20 *(e)*).

Case 4. May a player jump over the net into his opponent's Court while the ball is in play and not suffer penalty?

Decision. No. He loses the point (Rule 20 *(e)*).

Case 5. A cuts the ball just over the net, and it returns to A's side. B, unable to reach the ball, throws his racket and hits the ball. Both racket and ball fall over the net on A's Court. A returns the ball outside of B's Court. Does B win or lose the point?

Decision. B loses the point (Rule 20 *(e)* and *(h)*).

Case 6. A player standing outside the service Court is struck by a service ball before it has touched the ground. Does he win or lose the point?

Decision. The player struck loses the point (Rule 20 *(g)*), except as provided under Rule 14 *(a)*.

Case 7. A player standing outside the Court volleys the ball or catches it in his hand and claims the point because the ball was certainly going out of court.

Decision. In no circumstances can he claim the point:

(1) If he catches the ball he loses the point under Rule 20 *(g)*.

(2) If he volleys it and makes a bad return he loses the point under Rule 20 *(c)*.

(3) If he volleys it and makes a good return, the rally continues.

RULE 21

Player Hinders 0opponent

If a player commits any act which hinders his opponent in making a stroke, then, if this is deliberate, he shall lose the point or if involuntary, the point shall be replayed.

> **USTA Comment:** *'Deliberate' means a player did what he intended to do, although the resulting effect on his opponent might or might not have been what he intended. Example: a player, after his return is in the air, gives advice to his partner in such a loud voice that his opponent is hindered. 'Involuntary' means a non-intentional act such as a hat blowing off or a scream resulting from a sudden wasp sting.*
>
> **USTA Comment:** *Upon appeal by a competitor that the server's action in discarding a "second ball" after a rally has started constitutes a distraction (hindrance), the Umpire, if he deems the claim valid, shall require the server to make some other satisfactory disposition of the ball. Failure to comply with this instruction shall result in loss of a point on each occasion.*

Case 1. Is a player liable to a penalty if in making a stroke he touches his opponent?

Decision. No, unless the Umpire deems it necessary to take action under Rule 21.

Case 2. When a ball bounds back over the net the player concerned may reach over the net in order to play the ball. What is the ruling if the player is hindered from doing this by his opponent?

Decision. In accordance with Rule 21, the Umpire may either award the point to the player hindered, or order the point to be replayed. (See also Rule 25.)

Case 3. Does an involuntary double hit constitute an act which hinders an opponent within Rule 21?
Decision. No.

RULE 22

Ball Falls on Line

A ball falling on a line is regarded as falling in the Court bounded by that line.

> **USTA Comment:** *In a non-officiated match, each player makes the call on any ball hit toward his side of the net. If a player cannot call a ball out with surety he should regard it as good. In doubles, normally the Receiver's partner makes the calls with respect to the service line, with the Receiver calling the side and center lines, but either partner may make the call on any ball he clearly sees out.*

RULE 23

Ball Touches Permanent Fixtures

If the ball in play touches a permanent fixture (other than the net, posts, singles sticks, cord or metal cable, strap or band) after it has hit the ground, the player who struck it wins the point; if before it hits the ground, his opponent wins the point.

> **USTA Comment:** *A ball in play that after passing the net strikes a pipe support running across the court at the base of the net is regarded the same as a ball landing on clear ground. See USTA Comment under Rule 20 (e) for a player who touches a pipe support.*

Case 1. A return hits the Umpire or his chair or stand. The player claims that the ball was going into Court.
Decision. He loses the point.

RULE 24

A Good Return

It is a good return:

(a) If the ball touches the net, posts, singles sticks, cord or metal cable, strap or band, provided that it passes over any of them and hits the ground within the Court; or

(b) If the ball, served or returned, hits the ground within the proper Court and rebounds or is blown back over the net, and the player whose turn it is to strike reaches over the net and plays the ball, provided that he does not contravene Rule 20(e), and that the stroke be otherwise good; or

(c) If the ball is returned outside the posts, or singles sticks, either above or below the level of the top of the net, even though it touches the posts or singles sticks, provided that it hits the ground within the proper Court; or

(d) If a player's racket passes over the net after he has returned the ball, provided the ball passes the net before being played and is properly returned; or

(e) If a player succeeds in returning the ball, served or in play, which strikes a ball lying in the Court.

> **USTA Comment:** *Paragraph (e) of the rule refers to a ball lying on the court at the start of the point, as a result of a service let or fault, or as a result of a player dropping it. If a ball in play strikes a rolling or stationary "foreign" ball that has come from elsewhere after the point started, a let should be played. See Case 7 under Rule 25 which pertains to an object other than a ball that is being used in the match.*

ITF Note: In a singles match, if, for the sake of convenience, a doubles court is equipped with singles sticks for the purpose of a singles game, then the doubles posts and those portions of the net, cord or metal cable and the band outside such singles sticks shall at all times be permanent fixtures, and are not regarded as posts or parts of the net of a singles game.

A return that passes under the net cord between the singles stick and adjacent doubles post without touching either net cord, net or doubles post and falls within the court, is a good return.

> **USTA Comment:** *In doubles this would be a "through"—loss of point.*

Case 1. A ball going out of Court hits a net post or singles stick and falls within the lines of the opponent's Court. Is the stroke good?
Decision. If a service; no, under Rule 10 *(c)*. If other than a service: yes, under Rule 24 *(a)*.
Case 2. Is it a good return if a player returns the ball holding his racket in both hands?
Decision. Yes.
Case 3. The service or ball in play, strikes a ball lying in the Court. Is the point won or lost thereby?

> **USTA Comment:** *A ball that is touching a boundary line is considered to be "lying in The court."*

Decision. No. Play must continue. If it is not clear to the Umpire that the right ball is returned a let should be called.
Case 4. May a player use more than one racket at any time during play?
Decision. No; the whole implication of the Rules is singular.
Case 5. May a player request that a ball or balls lying in his opponent's court be removed?
Decision. Yes, but not while a ball is in play.

> **USTA Comment:** *This request must be honored.*

RULE 25

Hindrance of a Player

In case a player is hindered in making a stroke by anything not within his control, except a permanent fixture of the Court, or except as provided for in Rule 21, a let shall be called.

> **USTA Comment:** *See Rule 13 and its USTA Comments regarding lets.*

Case 1. A spectator gets into the way of a player, who fails to return the ball. May the player then claim a let?
Decision. Yes, if in the Umpire's opinion he was obstructed by circumstances beyond his control, but not if due to permanent fixtures of the Court or the arrangements of the ground.
Case 2. A player is interfered with as in Case No. 1, and the Umpire calls a let. The Server had previously served a fault. Has he the right to two services?
Decision. Yes: as the ball is in play, the point, not merely the stroke, must be replayed as the Rule provides.
Case 3. May a player claim a let under Rule 25 because he thought his opponent was being hindered, and consequently did not expect the ball to be returned?
Decision. No.
Case 4. Is a stroke good when a ball in play hits another ball in the air?
Decision. A let should be called unless the other ball is in the air by the act of one of the players, in which case the Umpire will decide under Rule 21.
Case 5. If an Umpire or other judge erroneously calls "fault" or "out", and then corrects himself, which of the calls shall prevail?
Decision. A let must be called unless, in the opinion of the Umpire, neither player is hindered in his game, in which case the corrected call shall prevail.
Case 6. If the first ball served — a fault — rebounds, interfering with the Receiver at the time of the second service, may the Receiver claim a let?

Decision. Yes. But if he had an opportunity to remove the ball from the Court and negligently failed to do so, he may not claim a let.

Case 7. Is it a good stroke if the ball touches a stationary or moving object on the Court?

Decision. It is a good stroke unless the stationary object came into Court after the ball was put into play in which case a let must be called. If the ball in play strikes an object moving along or above the surface of the Court a let must be called.

Case 8. What is the ruling if the first service is a fault, the second service correct, and it becomes necessary to call a let either under the provision of Rule 25 or if the Umpire is unable to decide the point?

Decision. The fault shall be annulled and the whole point replayed.

RULE 26

Score in a Game

If a player wins his first point, the score is called 15 for that player; on winning his second point, the score is called 30 for that player; on winning his third point, the score is called 40 for that player, and the fourth point won by a player is scored game for that player except as below:

If both players have won three points, the score is called deuce; and the next point won by a player is scored advantage for that player. If the same player wins the next point, he wins the game; if the other player wins the next point the score is again called deuce; and so on, until a player wins the two points immediately following the score at deuce, when the game is scored for that player.

> **USTA Comment:** *In a non-officiated match the Server should announce, in a voice audible to his opponent and spectators, the set score at the beginning of each game, and point scores as the game goes on. Misunderstandings will be avoided if this practice is followed.*

RULE 27

Score in a Set

(a) A player (or players) who first wins six games wins a set; except that he must win by a margin of two games over his opponent and where necessary a set is extended until this margin is achieved.

(b) The tie-break system of scoring may be adopted as an alternative to the advantage set system in paragraph (a) of this Rule provided the decision is announced in advance of the match.

In this case, the following Rules shall be effective:

The tie-break shall operate when the score reaches six games all in any set except in the third or fifth set of a three set or five set match respectively when an ordinary advantage set shall be played, unless otherwise decided and announced in advance of the match.

The following system shall be used in a tie-break game.

Singles

(i) A player who first wins seven points shall win the game and the set provided he leads by a margin of two points. If the score reaches six points all the game shall be extended until this margin had been achieved. Numerical scoring shall be used throughout the tie-break game.

(ii) The player whose turn it is to serve shall be the server for the first point. His opponent shall be the server for the second and third points and thereafter each player shall serve alternately for two consecutive points until the winner of the game and set has been decided.

(iii) From the first point, each service shall be delivered alternately from the right and left courts, beginning from the right court. If service from a wrong half of the court occurs and is undetected, all play resulting from such wrong service or services shall stand, but the inaccuracy of station shall be corrected immediately it is discovered.

(iv) Players shall change ends after every six points and at the conclusion of the tie-break game.

(v) The tie-break game shall count as one game for the ball change, except that, if the balls are due to be changed at the beginning of the tie-break, the change shall be delayed until the second game of the following set.

Doubles

In doubles the procedure for singles shall apply. The player whose turn it is to serve shall be the server for the first point. Thereafter each player shall serve in rotation for two points, in the same order as previously in that set, until the winners of the game and set have been decided.

Rotation of Service

The player (or pair in the case of doubles) whose turn it was to serve first in the tie-break game shall receive service in the first game of the following set.

Case 1. At six all the tie-break is played, although it has been decided and announced in advance of the match that an advantage set will be played. Are the points already played counted?

Decision. If the error is discovered before the ball is put in play for the second point, the first point shall count but the error shall be corrected immediately. If the error is discovered after the ball is put in play for the second point the game shall continue as a tie-break game.

Case 2. At six all, an advantage game is played, although it has been decided and announced in advance of the match that a tie-break will be played. Are the points already played counted?

Decision. If the error is discovered before the ball is put in play for the second point, the first point shall be counted but the error shall be corrected immediately. If the error is discovered after the ball is put in play for the second point an advantage set shall be continued. If the score thereafter reaches eight games all or a higher even number, a tie-break shall be played.

Case 3. If during a tie-break in a singles or doubles game, a player serves out of turn, shall the order of service remain as altered until the end of the game?

Decision. If a player has completed his turn of service the order of service shall remain as altered. If the error is discovered before a player has completed his turn of service the order of service shall be corrected immediately and any points already played shall count.

RULE 28

Maximum Number of Sets

The maximum number of sets in a match shall be 5, or, where women take part, 3.

RULE 29

Role of Court Officials

In matches where an Umpire is appointed, his decision shall be final; but where a Referee is appointed, an appeal shall lie to him from the decision of an Umpire on a question of law, and in all such cases the decision of the Referee shall be final.

In matches where assistants to the Umpire are appointed (Linesmen, Net-cord Judges, Foot-fault Judges) their decisions shall be final on questions of fact except that if in the opinion of an Umpire a clear mistake has been made he shall have the right to change the decision of an assistant or order a let to be played. When such an assistant is unable to give a decision he shall indicate this immediately to the Umpire who shall give a decision. When an Umpire is unable to give a decision on a question of fact he shall order a let to be played.

In Davis Cup matches or other team competitions where a Referee is on Court, any decision can be changed by the Referee, who may also instruct an Umpire to order a let to be played.

The Referee, in his discretion, may at any time postpone a match on account of darkness or the condition of the ground or the weather. In any case of postponement the previous score and previous occupancy of Courts shall hold good, unless the Referee and the players unanimously agree otherwise.

USTA Comment: *See third USTA Comment under Rule 30 regarding resumption of suspended match.*

Case 1. The Umpire orders a let, but a player claims that the point should not be replayed. May the Referee be requested to give a decision?

Decision. Yes. A question of tennis law, that is an issue relating to the application of specific facts, shall first be determined by the Umpire. However, if the Umpire is uncertain or if a player appeals from his determination, then the Referee shall be requested to give a decision, and his decision is final.

Case 2. A ball is called out but a player claims that the ball was good. May the Referee give a ruling?

Decision. No. This is a question of fact that is an issue relating to what actually occurred during a specific incident, and the decision of the on-court officials is therefore final.

Case 3. May an Umpire overrule a Linesman at the end of a rally if, in his opinion, a clear mistake has been made during the course of a rally?

Decision. No, unless in his opinion the opponent was hindered. Otherwise an Umpire may only overrule a Linesman if he does so immediately after the mistake has been made .

USTA Comment: *See Rule 17, Case 1 regarding non-officiated matches.*

Case 4. A Linesman calls a ball out. The Umpire was unable to see clearly, although he thought the ball was in. May he overrule the Linesman?

Decision. No. An Umpire may only overrule if he considers that a call was incorrect beyond all reasonable doubt. He may only overrule a ball determined good by a Linesman if he has been able to see a space between the ball and the line; and he may only overrule a ball determined out, or a fault, by a Linesman if he has seen the ball hit the line or fall inside the line.

Case 5. May a Linesman change his call after the Umpire has given the score?

Decision. Yes. If a Linesman realizes he has made an error, he may make a correction provided he does so immediately.

Case 6. A player claims his return shot was good after a Linesman called "out." May the Umpire overrule the Linesman?

Decision. No. An Umpire may never overrule as a result of a protest or an appeal by a player.

RULE 30

Continuous Play and Rest Periods

Play shall be continuous from the first service until the match is concluded, in accordance with the following provisions:

(a) If the first service is a fault, the second service must be struck by the Server without delay.

The Receiver must play to the reasonable pace of the Server and must be ready to receive when the Server is ready to serve.

When changing ends a maximum of one minute thirty seconds shall elapse from the moment the ball goes out of play at the end of the game to the time the ball is struck for the first point of the next game.

The Umpire shall use his discretion when there is interference which makes it impractical for play to be continuous.

The organizers of international circuits and team events recognized by the ITF may determine the time allowed between points, which shall not at any time exceed 25 seconds.

USTA Comment: *When practical, in USTA sanctioned tournaments using a certified official in direct observation of the match, the time which shall elapse from the moment the ball goes out of play at the end of the point to the time the ball is struck shall not exceed 25 seconds.*

(b) Play shall never be suspended, delayed or interfered with for the purpose of enabling a player to recover his strength, breath, or physical condition.

However, in the case of accidental injury, the Umpire may allow a one-time three minute suspension for that injury.

The organizers of international circuits and team events recognized by the ITF may extend the one-time suspension period from three minutes to five minutes.

(c) If, through circumstances outside the control of the player, his clothing, footwear or equipment (excluding racket) becomes out of adjustment in such a way that it is impossible or undesirable for him to play on, the Umpire may suspend play while the maladjustment is rectified.

USTA Comment: *Loss of, or damage to, a contact lens or eyeglasses shall be treated as equipment maladjustment. All players must follow the same rules with respect to suspending play, even though in misty, but playable, weather a player who wears glasses may be handicapped.*

(d) The Umpire may suspend or delay play at any time as may be necessary and appropriate.

USTA Comment: *When a match is resumed after a suspension of more than ten minutes, the players may engage in a re-warm-up that may be of the same duration as that at the start of the match. The preferred method is to warm-up with other used balls and then insert the match balls when play starts. If the match balls are used in the re-warm-up, then the next ball change will be two games sooner. There shall be no re-warm-up after an authorized intermission or after a suspension of ten minutes or less.*

(e) After the third set, or when women take part the second set, either player is entitled to a rest, which shall not exceed 10 minutes, or in countries situated between latitude 15 degrees north and latitude 15 degrees south, 45 minutes and furthermore, when necessitated by circumstances not within the control of the players, the Umpire may suspend play for such a period as he may consider necessary. If play is suspended and is not resumed until a later day the rest may be taken only after the third set (or when women take part the second set) of play on such a later day, completion of an unfinished set being counted as one set.

If play is suspended and is not resumed until 10 minutes have elapsed in the same day the rest may be taken only after three consecutive sets have been played without interruption (or when women take part two sets), completion of an unfinished set being counted as one set.

Any nation and/or committee organizing a tournament, match or competition, other than the International Tennis Championships (Davis Cup and Federation Cup), is at liberty to modify this provision or omit it from its regulations provided this is announced before the event commences.

(f) A tournament committee has the discretion to decide the time allowed for a warm-up period prior to a match but this may not exceed five minutes and must be announced before the event commences.

USTA Comment: *When there are no ballpersons this time may be extended to 10 minutes.*

(g) When approved point penalty and non-accumulative point penalty systems are in operation, the Umpire shall make his decisions within the terms of those systems.

(h) Upon violation of the principle that play shall be continuous the Umpire may, after giving due warning, disqualify the offender.

RULE 31

Coaching

During the playing of a match in a team competition, a player may receive coaching from a captain who is sitting on the court only when he changes ends at the end of a game, but not when he changes ends during a tie-break game.

A player may not receive coaching during the playing of any other match.

After due warning an offending player may be disqualified. When an approved point penalty system is in operation, the Umpire shall impose penalties according to that system.

Case 1. Should a warning be given or the player be disqualified, if the coaching is given by signals in an unobtrusive manner?

Decision. The Umpire must take action as soon as he becomes aware that coaching is being given verbally or by signals. If the Umpire is unaware that coaching is being given, a player may draw his attention to the fact that advice is being given.

Case 2. Can a player receive coaching during an authorized rest period under Rule 30(e), or when play is interrupted and he leaves the court?

Decision. Yes. In these circumstances, when the player is not on the court, there is no restriction on coaching.

ITF Note: The word "coaching" includes any advice or instruction.

RULE 32

Changing Balls

In cases where balls are to be changed after a specified number of games, if the balls are not changed in the correct sequence, the mistake shall be corrected when the player or pair in the case of doubles who should have served with new balls is next due to serve. Thereafter the balls shall be changed so that the number of games between changes shall be that originally agreed.

RULE 33

The Doubles Game

The above Rules shall apply to the Doubles Game except as below.

RULE 34

The Doubles Court

For the Doubles Game, the Court shall be 36 feet (10.97m) in width, i.e. 4½ feet (1.37m) wider on each side than the Court for the Singles Game, and those portions of the singles side-lines which lie between the two service-lines shall be called the service side-lines. In other respects, the Court shall be similar to that described in Rule 1, but the portions of the singles side-lines between the base-line and service-line on each side of the net may be omitted if desired.

> **USTA Comment:** *The Server has the right in doubles to stand anywhere back of the baseline between the center mark imaginary extension and the doubles sideline imaginary extension.*

RULE 35

Order of Service in Doubles

The order of serving shall be decided at the beginning of each set as follows:

The pair who have to serve in the first game of each set shall decide which partner shall do so and the opposing pair shall decide similarly for the second game. The partner of the player who served in the first game shall serve in the third; the partner of the player who served in the second game shall serve in the fourth, and so on in the same order in all the subsequent games of a set.

Case 1. In doubles, one player does not appear in time to play, and his partner claims to be allowed to play single-handed against the opposing players. May he do so?

Decision. No.

RULE 36

Order of Receiving in Doubles

The order of receiving the service shall be decided at the beginning of each set as follows:

The pair who have to receive the service in the first game shall decide which partner shall receive the first service, and that partner shall continue to receive the first service in every odd game throughout that set. The opposing pair shall likewise decide which partner shall receive the first service in the second game and that partner shall continue to receive the first service in every even game throughout that set. Partners shall receive the service alternately throughout each game.

Case 1. Is it allowable in doubles for the Server's partner or the Receiver's partner to stand in a position that obstructs the view of the Receiver?

Decision. Yes. The Server's partner or the Receiver's partner may take any position on his side of the net in or out of the Court that he wishes.

RULE 37

Service Out of Turn in Doubles

If a partner serves out of his turn, the partner who ought to have served shall serve as soon as the mistake is discovered, but all points scored, and any faults served before such discovery, shall be reckoned. If a game shall have been completed before such discovery, the order of service remains as altered.

> **USTA Comment:** *For an exception to Rule 37 see Case 3 under Rule 27.*

RULE 38

Error in Order of Receiving in Doubles

If during a game the order of receiving the service is changed by the Receivers it shall remain as altered until the end of the game in which the mistake is discovered, but the partners shall resume their original order of receiving in the next game of that set in which they are Receivers of the service.

RULE 39

Service Fault in Doubles

The service is a fault as provided for by Rule 10, or if the ball touches the Server's partner or anything which he wears or carries; but if the ball served touches the partner of the Receiver, or anything which he wears or carries, not being a let under Rule 14(a) before it hits the ground, the Server wins the point.

RULE 40

Playing the Ball in Doubles

The ball shall be struck alternately by one or other player of the opposing pairs, and if a player touches the ball in play with his racket in contravention of this Rule, his opponents win the point.

> **USTA Comment:** *The partners themselves do not have to "alternate" in making returns. In the course of making one return, only one member of a doubles team may hit the ball. If both of them hit the ball, either simultaneously or consecutively, it is an illegal return. Mere clashing of rackets does not make a return illegal unless it is clear that more than one racket touched the ball.*

ITF Note: Except where otherwise stated, every reference in these rules to the masculine includes the feminine gender.

If you have a rules problem, send full details, enclosing a stamped self-addressed envelope to USTA Tennis Rules Committee, c/o Officials' Department, 70 West Red Oak Lane, White Plains, NY 10604.

APPENDIX I

Regulations for Making Tests Specified in Rule 3

1. Unless otherwise specified all tests shall be made at a temperature of approximately 68° Fahrenheit (20° Centigrade) and a relative humidity of approximately 60 per cent. All balls should be removed from their container and kept at the recognized temperature and humidity for 24 hours prior to testing, and shall be at that temperature and humidity when the test is commenced.

2. Unless otherwise specified the limits are for a test conducted in an atmospheric pressure resulting in a barometric reading of approximately 30 inches (76cm.).

3. Other standards may be fixed for localities where the average temperature, humidity or average barometric pressure at which the game is being played differ materially from 68° Fahrenheit (20° Centigrade), 60 per cent and 30 inches (76cm.) respectively.

   Applications for such adjusted standards may be made by any National Association to the International Tennis Federation and if approved shall be adopted for such localities.

4. In all tests for diameter a ring gauge shall be used consisting of a metal plate, preferably non-corrosive, of a uniform thickness of one-eighth of an inch (.32cm.) in which there are two circular openings 2.575 inches (6.54cm.) and 2.700 inches (6.86cm.) in diameter respectively. The inner surface of the gauge shall have a convex profile with a radius of one-sixteenth of an inch (.16cm.). The ball shall not drop through the smaller opening by its own weight and shall drop through the larger opening by its own weight.

5. In all tests for deformation conducted under Rule 3, the machine designed by Percy Herbert Stevens and patented in Great Britain under Patent No. 230250, together with the subsequent additions and improvements thereto, including the modifications required to take return deformations, shall be employed or such other machine which is approved by a National Association and gives equivalent readings to the Stevens machine.

6. Procedure for carrying out tests.

   (a) Pre-compression. Before any ball is tested it shall be steadily compressed by approximately one inch (2.54cm.) on each of three diameters at right angles to one another in succession; this process to be carried out three times (nine compressions in all). All tests to be completed within two hours of precompression.

   (b) Bound test (as in Rule 3). Measurements are to be taken from the concrete base to the bottom of the ball.

   (c) Size test (as in paragraph 4 above).

   (d) Weight test (as in Rule 3).

   (e) Deformation test. The ball is placed in position on the modified Stevens machine so that neither platen of the machine is in contact with the cover seam. The contact weight is applied, the pointer and the mark brought level, and the dials set to zero. The test weight equivalent to 18 lb. (8.165kg.) is placed on the beam and pressure applied by turning the wheel at a uniform speed so that five seconds elapse from the instant the beam leaves its seat until the pointer is brought level with the mark. When turning ceases the reading is recorded (forward deformation). The wheel is turned again until figure ten is reached on the scale (one inch [2.54 cm.] deformation). The wheel is then rotated in the opposite direction at a uniform speed (thus releasing pressure) until the beam pointer again coincides with the mark. After waiting ten seconds the pointer is adjusted to the mark if necessary. The reading is then recorded (return

deformation). This procedure is repeated on each ball across the two diameters at right angles to the initial position and to each other.

APPENDIX II

Rules of Wheelchair Tennis

The Rules of Tennis shall apply to wheelchair tennis with the following exceptions:

1. The wheelchair player is allowed two bounces.
2. The first bounce must land inside the court boundaries.
3. Service must be initiated with both rear wheels behind the baseline.
4. The Chair is part of the body. All applicable rules apply.

   (a) A player loses the point if the ball in play touches him or his wheelchair or anything he wears or carries, except his racket in his hand(s). This loss of a point occurs regardless of whether the player is inside or outside the bounds of his court when the ball touches him.

   (b) The player loses the point if a served ball hits him or his wheelchair or anything he carries, except his racket in his hand(s). If the server hits his own partner with the served ball, then it is a fault.

   (c) A wheel fault is incurred if during the delivery of the service either of the rear wheels touches any area other than that behind the baseline within the imaginary extensions of the center mark and side lines. The front wheels may be situated over the baseline and/or center lines

Tie-Breaks and No-Ad Scoring

1) *Tie-Break Use Mandatory.* Use of the 12-point tie-break is mandatory in all sanctioned tournaments in all sets.

2) *Twelve-Point Tie-Break.*

   Singles: Player A, having served the first game of the set, serves the first point from the right court; Player B serves points 2 and 3 (left and right); A serves points 4 and 5 (left and right); B serves point 6 (left) and after they change ends, point 7 (right); A serves points 8 and 9 (left and right); B serves points 10 and 11 (left and right); A serves point 12 (left). A player who reaches seven points during these first 12 points wins the game and set. If the score has reached six points all, the players change ends and continue in the same pattern until one player establishes a margin of two points which gives him the game and set. Note that the players change ends every six points and that the player who serves the last point of one of these 6-point segments also serves the first point of the next one (from right court). For a following set the players change ends and B serves the first game.

   Doubles: The same pattern as in singles applies, with partners preserving their serving sequence. In a game of A-B versus C-D, with A having served the first game of the set, A serves the first point (right); C serves points 2 and 3 (left and right); B serves points 4 and 5 (left and right); D serves point 6 (left) and after the teams change ends, D serves point 7 (right); A serves points 8 and 9 (left and right); C serves points 10 and 11 (left and right); B serves point 12 (left) A team that wins seven points during these first 12 points wins the game and set. If the score has reached six points all, the teams change ends. B then serves point 13 (right), and they continue until one team establishes a two-point margin and thus wins the game and set. As in singles, they change ends for one game to start a following set, with team C-D to serve first.

3) *Experimental 12-point tie-break.* The experimental 12-point tie-break is the same as the present 12-point tie-break except that ends are changed after the first point, then after every four points, and at the conclusion of the tie-break game.

4) *When experimental 12-point tie-break is authorized.* For experimental purposes a section may authorize any tournament below the National Championship level to use the experimental 12-point tie-break. For experimental purposes, the USTA Sanctions and Schedules Committee may authorize the use of the experimental 12-point tie-break for any other tournament. Any tournament electing to use the experimental 12-point tie-break must announce the election before the start of tournament play.

5) *Recording the tie-break score.* The score of the tie-break set will be written 7-6(x) or 6-7(x), with (x) being the number of points won by the loser of the tie-break. For example, 7-6(4) means the tie-break score was 7-4, and 6-7(14) means the tie-break score was 14-16.

6) *Changing ends during the tie-break.* Changes of ends during a tie break game are to be made within the normal time allowed between points.

7) *Ball changes.* If a ball change is due on a tie-break game, it will be deferred until the start of the second game of the next set. A tie-break game counts as one game in determining ball changes.

8) *No-Ad scoring.* The No-Ad procedure is simply what the name implies: the first player to win four points wins the game, with the seventh point of a game becoming a game point for each player. The receiver has the choice of advantage court or deuce court to which the service is to be delivered on the seventh point. No-ad scoring is authorized for tournaments at the sectional championship level and below. A tournament electing to use no-ad scoring must announce the election before the start of tournament play except as set forth in paragraph 9 below.

Note: The score-calling may be either in the conventional terms or in simple numbers, i e, "zero, one, two, three, game."

Cautionary Note: Any ITF-authorized tournament should get special authorization from ITF before using No-Ad.

9) *Change to No-Ad scoring.* The referee can switch to no-ad scoring from regular scoring in any round without prior notice on the entry blank when in the referee's discretion the change is necessary to complete the tournament after inclement weather or other factors cause the tournament to fall behind its published schedule.

Printed with permission of the USTA.

Index